Head and Face Masks in Navajo Ceremonialism

Head and Face Masks in Navaho Ceremonialism

Berard Haile

University of Utah Press
Salt Lake City

∞ Printed on acid-free paper

Originally published in 1947 by the St. Michaels Press.

Library of Congress Cataloging-in-Publication Data

Haile, Berard, 1874–1961.
Head and face masks in Navaho ceremonialism / Berard Haile.
p. cm.
Originally published: St. Michaels, Ariz. : St. Michaels Press, 1947.
Includes bibliographical references.
ISBN 0-87480-504-X (alk. paper)
1. Navajo masks. 2. Night Chant (Navajo rite) 3. Navajo Indians—Rites and ceremonies. I. Title.
E99.N3H23 1996
299'.782—dc20 95-46996

To my Navaho friends

past and present

this monograph is respectfully dedicated.

Contents

Illustrations

Acknowledgments

The field work and research that resulted in this monograph were undertaken upon my own initiative. Its publication however was made possible by a list of generous prepublication subscribers. To these I am indebted. I also received personal encouragement to go ahead with the publication from Frederick Webb Hodge of the Southwest Museum, Los Angeles, Harry Hoijer of UCLA, Clyde Kluckhohn, Mary C. Wheelwright, and others.

I am particularly indebted to E. Leslie Eames of Los Angeles, California, for combinations reproduced in colored transparencies that greatly facilitated the study and engraving of the colored product. The originals of the first informant were most faithfully redrawn by a nun artist who asks not to be mentioned by name. I respect her wishes and appreciate her valuable contribution to the monograph.

Among my Indian friends who have contributed data, drawings, suggestions, opinions on disputed points, and the like, I cherish and hold the memory of those who are gone before me and cherish the conviction that I have true friends among those who are still living. I need not mention these by name.

Foreword

Father Berard Haile's *Head and Face Masks in Navaho Ceremonialism* was initially published in 1947 by the Franciscan Friars' small St. Michaels Press in an edition of only five hundred—each with fourteen hand-tipped, silk-screened reproductions of masks.[1] This reprinting joins a distinguished series of reprintings of classical works on Navajo belief systems and ceremonialism newly inaugurated by the University of Utah Press, and is to be welcomed for many reasons. It is the only text that accounts for the origins of the *yé'ii* (ontologically, not locationally[2]). Second, it is the

---

[1]In the original edition were three photographs of the mask set purchased by St. Michaels in 1910 (see p. 82). These are not reproduced here in deference to contemporary Navajo views of the public display of actual Nightway masks or their photographs. The spelling "Navaho," used by Fr. Berard and anthropologists of the time, has now of course been replaced by "Navajo." Fr. Berard did not adopt the "h" spelling out of fashion, however, and was far less wedded to it than Matthews, Kluckhohn, Vogt, Wyman and others (see Haile, 1949).

[2]This is somewhat unfortunate, for the actual locational specifity of the relevant *yé'ii* is one of the important factors in Nightway branch designations and has yet to be systematically assembled.

most detailed account of the necessary attributes and construction of Navajo masks (surpassing even Washington Matthews's grand 1902 volume—reprinted in 1995 by the University of Utah Press). It provides a good composite generalized account of the nine-day Nightway healing practice, day by day (with occasional concrete additions from one or another specific Nightway *hataałii*). It also details a historical account of one specific Nightway mask set (with genealogies of practitioners).[3] Finally, it presents, in Navajo as well as interlinear English translation (and also free translation), about half of the opening prayer of the Nightway's last night initial dancers' appearance. In addition, it has an extended discussion of two masks and their ceremony (and ontology) whose existence is disputed. These latter two Fr. Berard assigns to a portion of Upward Reaching Way, no longer practiced (see Haile, 1981).

What we have before us is a remarkable work in which Fr. Berard reports what he was told with a minimum of interpretation, explanation, redaction. He makes few assumptions, and here seldom extends an opinion beyond the facts at his disposal. He hints at Western projects ("To trace the provenience of Navaho masks would require an extensive comparative study of masks found elsewhere" [p. xxii), but thankfully does not undertake them, and gives us instead a *Navajo account* of the origin of the *yé'ii*, something no other publication has done.

The volume has a disarmingly analytical and very literal character. For example, Fr. Berard is very careful to title the volume "Head *and* Face Masks in Navaho Ceremonialism," telling readers that he intends to

---

[3]This distinguished mask set was still (as of 1990) at the St. Michaels mission, but access was strictly limited. The set was badly in need of conservation and should best be returned to the Navajo. The Ned Hatathli Cultural Center Museum of the Navajo Community College at Tsaile, AZ, has an excellent repatriation program for such sacred material, which attempts to get masks back into the medicine bundles of healers.

deal with masks that cover the head as well as those that only cover the face. To most speakers of English, the word "mask" could easily be understood to include both types, and the volume could have been simply "Masks in Navaho Ceremonialism." Again, he does not assume readers will understand that the figures in the sandpaintings are the same as those impersonated with masks—so he tells us—though I cannot see how even those most casually familiar with Navajo healing would not know that the *yé'ii* in the sandpaintings and the *yé'ii* that appear as masked God Impersonators are the same.

Perhaps such an approach to the subject, however, also accounts for the fact that the syntax is cumbersome and frequently confusing. The volume could have benefited enormously from a careful editing. For example, there are sentences like, "Both sandpainting figures and masked impersonators are identified with the supernaturals themselves, and visualize that they enter the hogan in person (p. xxii)." I assume that the portion after the comma in this sentence means that the masked impersonators see themselves as personifying the Holy People when they enter the medicine hogan. But it is not very clear to me what is actually meant.

Much of the material was collected in the early part of the century (particularly from Cane's Son on the origin of the *yé'ii* in 1908), with only occasional updates and more recent data (from Slim Curley in 1934 and Nightway accounts from Slim Curley and Beadway Singer). Thus, there is an occasional reference to a contradiction or a confusion that subsequently came from another informant and that Fr. Berard is unable to resolve. Moreover, he acknowledges his reliance on an interpreter in the early collections. Indeed, Fr. Berard later preferred to collect entirely vernacular texts. These were never collected in actual healing contexts, however, and some distortion or change is to be expected (see Faris, 1994, for some of the problems of assembling texts out of context).[4]

Fr. Berard Haile was, of course, a devout Christian, a Franciscan, a mendicant (whose vows against property sometimes caused later scholars some difficulty in securing access to his materials (cf. Wyman, 1970; Haile, 1981). There was elsewhere some attempt to force Navajo belief systems into Western universalist schemes, but in general, even here, he considered them as discourses with a logic to be revealed and subject to authoritative scrutiny.[5] In this he was no different from almost every other Westerner who has examined Navajo belief complexes and healing systems. And he was a great deal more careful and respectful than the vast majority of scholars of the time. There is abundant evidence, including the present book, that he admired his Navajo collaborators very much, treated them as the professionals they were with many years of training and experience, had firm and close friendships with many people, especially some medicine men, and had great respect for Navajo healing

---

[4]Of course, for texts on the origin and ontology of the *yé'ii*, there is no healing context.

[5]In other works his Western origins leap forward. For example in Haile, 1943:65, he treats Navajo "supernaturals" as causal in Navajo healing. While they were once causal, in the world as now occupied by Navajo, individuals are largely responsible for themselves and their healing—it is the living who must seek to reorder themselves. The *yé'ii* attend and bless, but they are no longer directly causal. And the "Holy People" are not "supernatural," they are simply no longer visible, and today occupy the various sacred areas of Navajoland. Fr. Berard located causality out of Navajo hands, perhaps because such otiose assignment is so characteristic of the social and cultural forms from which Westerners come. And in the same text (Haile, 1943:60), he also shares Western anthropological orthodoxy regarding the late entry of Navajo into the Southwest—contrary to Navajo wisdom.

traditions and the philosophical underpinnings. There is little romance in this attachment (unlike Kluckhohn, Wyman, Reichard), but there is nevertheless much sentiment. In many ways, it is difficult to comprehend anyone else doing the kind of work Fr. Berard did, or being allowed and able to do the kind of work he did.

This intimacy and firm familiarity, however, does not mean Fr. Berard considered Navajo healing on its own terms, for as noted, he did not. The care and detailed attention in this volume I think has more to do with his linguistic focus, experience, expertise, and even his pedantry, than with his willingness to accept the object of his investigation as adequate to its own task. As can be seen, the present volume is filled with Navajo (in Fr. Berard's peculiar orthography), for he sought to secure the most accurate rendering of Navajo terms, determine their exact range of possible meanings, and rigorously sought to explore their semantic domains and attempt to exhaust their fields of application.

Yet there is no evidence he sought healing by Navajo specialists—even though he suffered a stroke and was paralyzed for the last few years of his life.[6] To several Nightway medicine men whom I interviewed in the last decade, this paralysis could have indeed been the result of his attitude and disbelief—known in English as "yeibichai sickness"—resulting from an insufficiently pious disposition toward the Nightway by people exposed to it. The same medicine men also felt this way about the deafness of

---

[6]Not having been "sung over," however, at least reveals something of Fr. Berard's personal integrity concerning Navajo healing, for others (Wyman, Reichard, Kluckhohn) all anxiously participated and had healing practices arranged for them, even though they did not respect Navajo causality on its own terms, and despite their unctuousness, continued to tell us what Navajo views "really" meant. Fr. Berard had contempt for this disingenuousness.

Washington Matthews, the death of Kenneth Foster,[7] and always make inquiries with a perverse sense of humor about the state of my own health, eyesight, and hearing!

All the same, Fr. Berard's linguistic commitment was extraordinarily fortuitous, for it is actually, as I understand Navajo causality, proper and appropriate *speaking* that is one central feature to a long, healthy, and beautiful life. The directed wind (which of course language is) not only is critical to a Navajo sense of life, humanness, but also to an inner series of meanings and orders—or, as Fr. Berard put it elsewhere, one's soul (see Haile, 1943; and McNeley, 1981). For example, the *yé'ii* (without speech) discussed herein are vital to Navajo history but also instructive in their lack of language, and this helps us to understand the central importance of directed speech, of the wind of language, to proper humanity and to healing. Healing always involves a reordering that uses an abundance of speech forms—in the framework of prayers, songs, instructions—to restore holiness, order, and beauty.

Fr. Berard had hoped to bring out a large complete new "Night Chant" volume to supplement and include data missing in Matthews's grand 1902 account. He collaborated in this with the anthropological linguist, Edward Sapir, the anthropologist Harry Hoijer, and others, but the project began to founder when they discovered the data from Slim Curley were dramatically different from the materials collected from Hastiin Klah and other Nightway specialists (see Faris, 1990:59). Indeed, this, combined with World War II, the shortage of men, paper, money, and Sapir's

[7]Kenneth Foster was the Director of the Museum of Navajo Ceremonial Art (the Wheelwright Musem of the American Indian) who collaborated on the filming of a Nightway in 1963. By the end of the year, Kenneth Foster, the medicine man involved (Son of Slim Curley), and the person sung over (Rose Begay), were all dead.

illnesses and death in 1939 resulted in an abandonment of the project.[8] Sapir and Hoijer published some texts (Sapir and Hoijer, 1942), Hoijer's transcriptions of Hastiin Klah's Nightway songs still exist in manuscript (at the Wheelwright Museum, WM 3-1-4), and Fr. Berard decided to bring out some of his own materials in the present book. His Nightway sandpainting collections remained unpublished until Faris, 1990, and many of his materials still remain in manuscript (see Faris, 1990:25–75). Part of the incompatibility of the various accounts, songs, prayers, sandpaintings rest with the different traditions from which each of the Nightway singers came (see Faris, 1990:19), the different contexts in which the materials were elicited and given, and perhaps even different etiological factors concerning the various *yé'ii* evoked (their locational specificity, their availability, etc.). But this small volume is an essential cluster of Fr. Berard's material.

There *are* errors and mistakes. Talking God always carries an Abert squirrel skin bag, *not* a "fawn skin" bag (p. 18), and Fr. Berard makes no mention of Talking God's essential white buckskin wrap. There is confusion on the number of lightning symbols on Monster Slayer's face (four *vs.* five) and the side of the face on which these should appear (left *vs.* right) on pages 23 and 27. There is no mention of Humpbacked God's cherrywood cane, nor the bluebird nest on same, nor indeed why he wears the hump, nor what it contains. The central figure in the Black God sandpainting reproduction is on a moon, *not* a "sun" (p. 61), and there *are* alternative Black God sandpaintings, not simply "Black God on stars" (p. 60). Fr. Berard also leaves out the initiation of girls at a Nightway (which differs somewhat from the initiation of boys—pages 54 and 55).

---

[8]Readers should consult Lyon, 1987, for a very good and thorough biographical account of Fr. Berard, his relationships with Navajo and with other Western scholars of Navajo belief systems. There are several bibliographical essays on Fr. Berard, but Powell, 1961, is a beginning.

Moreover, some of this work is not likely to be of too much use in certain respects. It is a very esoteric and arcane volume. Not only are the origins of the *yé'ii* not very relevant to most *hataałii*, but neither is the discussion of the *'ałké' na'ashii* masks and ontology. The details of construction of Nightway masks, their use in other chantways, the illustrations, the generalized discussion of the sequence of activities of a total Nightway, and the portion of the first of the last night's outside prayer are going to be of most use to practitioners and students.

Fr. Berard suggests that Washington Matthews (1902) may be safely followed, but verification with the present work is not exactly easy, for apart from about half of the first of the last night prayers, there are only the mask descriptions to compare.[9] These latter are unfortunately the least satisfactory portion of Matthews (1902) as well. The first of the last night prayers (the *'atsáłeeh*), however, are generally comparable. Other Nightway prayers are contained in unpublished Haile manuscripts now in the University of Arizona Library Special Collections, many of them still untranslated.

It is due to the care and linguistic commitment with which Fr. Berard undertook his work that we have a view of the extraordinary complexity of one portion of the Navajo conceptual universe. Certainly it undermines attempts to dilute this universe into an easy color/directional/gender/seasonal/diurnal/temporal/moral series of axes, so characteristic of Jungian comparative work or other Western-derived classificatory schemes, and allows us to begin to see the incredible intricacy of the system. These intricacies, often baroque and elaborate, are the rhetorics so necessary for restoring order, for situating beauty, for achieving peace. They are rather like, say, the structures of composition in a work such as Bach's *The Musical Offering*, where the canonical intricacies are a way of taking a

---

[9]The prayer comparisons actually are to be found in Matthews, 1897:269-275. But see also Faris, 1990:73–74 for some corrections.

grand theme and elaborating a devotional structure about it—indeed, an offering, a sacrifice—to once again achieve concord, holiness, *hózhǫ́*.

Bibliography

Faris, James C. 1990. The Nightway. *A History and a History of Documentation of a Navajo Ceremonial.* Albuquerque, University of New Mexico Press.

Faris, James C. 1994. Context and Text: Navajo Nightway Textual History in the Hands of the West. *Resources for American Literary Study* 20(2):180–195.

Faris, James C., and Harry Walters. 1990. Navajo History: Some Implications of Contrasts of Navajo Ceremonial Discourse. *History and Anthropology* 5:1–18.

Haile, Berard, O.F.M. 1926. *A Manual of Navaho Grammar.* St. Michaels AZ. [Printed by Santa Fe New Mexican Publishing Corporation].

Haile, Berard, O.F.M. 1943. Soul Concepts of the Navaho. *Annali Lateranensi* VII:59–94.

Haile, Berard. 1946. *The Navaho Fire Dance. Or Corral Dance. A Brief Account of its Practice and Meaning.* St. Michaels AZ, St. Michaels Press.

Haile, Berard, O.F.M. 1949. Navaho or Navajo? *The Americas* 6(1):-85–90.

Haile, Berard, O.F.M. 1981. *The Upward Moving and Emergence Way. The* Gishin Biye' *Version.* Edited by Karl Luckert. Lincoln, University of Nebraska Press.

Lyon, William H. 1987. Ednishodi Yazhe: The Little Priest and the Understanding of Navajo Culture. *American Indian Culture and Research Journal* 11(1):1–41.

McNeley, James Kale. 1981. *Holy Wind in Navajo Philosophy*. Tucson, University of Arizona Press.

Matthews, Washington. 1902. *The Night Chant, A Navaho Ceremony*. Publications of the Hyde Southwestern Expedition. New York, Memoirs of the American Museum of Natural History, Whole Series Volume 6 (Anthropology Series Volume 5). Reprint. Salt Lake City, The University of Utah Press, 1995.

Powell, Donald M. 1961. A Preliminary Bibliography of the Published Writings of Berard Haile, O.F.M. *Kiva* 26(4):44–47.

Sapir, Edward, and Harry Hoijer. 1942. *Navaho Texts*. Iowa City, Linguistic Society of America.

Wyman, Leland C. 1970. *Blessingway. With Three Versions of the Myth Recorded and Translated from the Navajo by Father Berard Haile, O.F.M.* Tucson, University of Arizona Press.

Introduction

One of the main purposes of this monograph is to present data on 'Head and Face Masks in Navaho Ceremonialism' which was obtained some 40 years ago. These data were allowed to lie dormant throughout these years partly because I wished to learn more about Navaho masks and their use, partly too because other work interfered which allowed little time for gathering additional data.

It was thought best to present this data as the informant gave it especially since it represented the thought of a family of singers to wit: **xastˣi·n giši·ǹ** the late Mr Cane and his sons: **xatˣa·łi· yą́žíni›** Little Singer now dead, **xatˣa·łi· né·zini›** the late Tall Singer and their youngest brother **giši·ǹ biγe›ni›** the late Cane's Son now dead.

Two years after obtaining the data on masks from Cane's Son we were fortunate enough to purchase a set of ye-i bichai masks which had been made in 1874. This again added new material to the original data. We have mentioned this in chapter III. Recently we were fortunate enough to secure a photo for our frontispiece of this set, the arrangement of which was made at our direction.

A second objective which we had in mind was to show what use is made of masks in various ceremonials. To do this we had to draw upon much unpublished text material dealing with Navaho ceremonials. Dr Washington Matthews's Night Chant was consulted and followed to some extent. Where his account did not explain the importance and functions of some of the masks native informants had to be consulted. This method resulted in bringing out mooted points on certain procedures but on the whole helped to shed light upon the presence of certain masks in the set.

It also brought out the fact that informants feel that there is an intimate connection between sandpaintings and masks. In Nightway, for example, the figures of sandpaintings wear masks which closely resemble the buckskin head and face masks seen in ceremonials of this chantway. Both sandpainting figures and masked impersonators are identified with the supernaturals themselves, and visualize that they enter the hogan in person.

This also occurs in other ceremonials which lay down sandpaintings said by informants to represent the supernaturals appearing in the hogan. These are not thought of as being masked even when their faces are colored brown, blue or white. The colored faces present their 'looks' as they are in reality, just as the masks should present the 'real' looks of those supernaturals. It follows then that we can here limit ourselves to masks proper.

To trace the provenience of Navaho masks would require an extensive comparative study of masks found elsewhere. Our thought was to leave this study to other students and to present the data on Navaho masks as we found them. Hence our monograph is limited in this respect also.

In the final chapter data is presented on the **'ałké·' na·'aši·** masks as presented in Upward-reachingway. Little is known of these two masks and one hesitates to say whether sets of them are to be found in the tribe. They are too dangerous for the owner. But what little is told of them is incorporated in this monograph.

Chapter One

γé'i· xazlį́·'gi
On the Origin of the ye-i

The following account is not connected with a chantway. It was told by the late **gišì·ǹ biγe'** Cane's Son, separately from his **xa'nełnéhe·** Upward-reachingway story. As it mentions the nine people of that story he seems to have thought of it as part of this legend. (My notes of 1908 are not clear in all details).

The nine people consulted for the good of the future human race. A hogan was made of **xayołká·ł** dawn, **naxode·ƛi·ž** horizontal blue, **naxo·coi** evening twilight, **čaxałxe·ł** darkness. These were in the shape of sticks three finger tips in length which were set upright at the cardinal points by first-man, then leaned upon each other so as to form a small cone. This was not exactly **'ał-čį' de·z'ái,** the conical hogan, but had that shape. By blowing upon them four times he increased the size of the poles to the height of about five feet.

Then **ǹni'í·łka·d** he spread a robe of dawn in the east, of sky blue[1] in the south, of evening twilight in the west, of darkness in the north. Upon these he placed a white bead, a turquoise, an abalone, a jet stone, and in the center of them a red stone. (The MS. reads that previously 'he took out (of his pouch) a turquoise **ni·ƙéhé** face print in the shape of our present thumb nail, a white bead in the shape of our present index finger nail, an abalone like our middle finger nail, a jet like our fourth finger nail, a red stone like our little finger nail.' The sense of this is probably that these jewels were placed on the various robes just mentioned).

---

[1] Sky blue appears to be a more convenient term for Navaho naxode·ƛi·ž 'horizontal blue.' This phenomenon is usually mentioned as the color of the south and is not identified with the arch of the sky, as this is called yá diłxił

Now **biƙi'iyí·łka·d** he spread a dawn (sheet) over the whole, over this **(biƙináyí·łka·d)** he again spread an unwounded buckskin, over this a sheet of skyblue, then an unwounded buckskin, then a sheet of evening twilight and another unwounded buckskin,

---

'the dark upper' possibly because the skies are dark at night.

There is however a distinct feeling that all colors — white, blue, yellow, black — belong to the east. Here, in the waning period of sunset, one notices a distinct blue hue in the eastern horizon which eventually fades into a yellow sunset color and replaces blue in the east to south and west. Eventually too these various colors are no longer discernible in the east, but sunset yellow centers chiefly on the western horizon, then fades away in the evening twilight.

In reality then, as Navahos view these phenomena, neither 'horizontal' blue is exclusively discernible in the south, nor 'horizontal' yellow in the west. Both of these phenomena, with darkness below horizontal blue and dawn or light above horizontal yellow are primarily to be sought in the eastern skies. The late Tall Mustache of łe·γi' tˣó Spring in soil, Arizona, was a consistent exponent of this tenet and did not hesitate to claim 'that all colors belong to the east.'

The assignment by ceremonials of white to the east, he would say, and of blue to the south, yellow to the west, black or dark to the north, does not alter the fact that the phenomena of these colors originate in the eastern skies. We notice color changes there first, meaning that we learn of horizon color changes from hues reflected on the eastern horizon after sunset and, before sunrise, on the western horizon.

This phenomenon leaves south and north cardinal points out of the reckoning, if one wishes to account for color assignments in the Navaho ceremonial complex.

This seems to be a sensible view to take of the variants which we find in Navaho ceremonials. Some assign black to the east, ignore white for this cardinal point, then skip over to west. East and west are the main cardinal points regardless of color.

Or we get a sunwise sequence east to south to west and north with the prevailing white, blue, yellow, black sequence. White or black may be assigned to the east, yellow to the west, blue to the south, pink or black to the north. On assignment of colors, then, east and north show greater divergence than do south (blue), west (yellow).

On phenomena the most general assignment is xayołká·ł dawn to the east, naxode·ƚi·ž horizontal blue to the south, naxo·coi horizontal yellow to the west, čaxałxe·ł darkness to the north. This assignment of phenomena is common in most ceremonials regardless and in spite of color assignments in prayersticks and sandpaintings. Usually pink color is assigned to north figures or sticks.

Here the assignment of phenomena and colors follows the usual pattern of Navaho ceremonialism. The jewels too, mentioned here, follow this pattern.

then a sheet of darkness and another unwounded buckskin, making eight covers all told.

Then he sprinkled water upon them, in the east from a **tˣósa·ˀ (tˣó ˀósa·ˀ) łagai** white waterpot, in the south water from **tˣósa·ˀ do·ƛiž** a blue pot, in the west water from **tˣósa·ˀ łico** a yellow pot, and in the north water from **tˣósa·ˀ diłxił** a dark waterpot. It appears that this symbolized the moisture which was introduced into their bodies in the shape of **tˣóžó·l nestˣi·ngo** a fine spray of water. He repeated the same with water from a **céłčíˀi· tˣósa·ˀ** a red stone waterpot, to infuse blood into the bodies.

He also owned **xadaxoniγeˀ łagai** white, blue, yellow, **diłxiłgo nodǫ́·z** dark striped, and **xadaxoniγeˀ łičí·ˀ** red mirage stone, the latter for the center. He blew on these stones or over them towards their respective water pots, which caused white, blue, yellow and **ƙos diłxiłgo nodǫ́·z** dark striped cloud, and red cloud to hover over the pots of these colors. This in turn caused the water to stir within the pots. The mirage stones here mentioned were symbolic of future clouds **ƙos łagai** etc. **do·lełgo ˀálˀį̨ ǯin** 'they say this was made for the future white (and other colored) clouds to be.'

When the clouds and water pots were in good working order first-man removed the covers, blew over them, then replaced them, an operation which he repeated four times. At the fourth uncovering, behold **xaščéłtˣiˀí** talking god appeared, and **xaščé-ˀo·γa·n** calling god, and **xaščé bˣką̨ˀ** male god, and **xaščé baˀá·d** female god, and **xaščé ˀołƫohí** shooting god, and **xá·da·či·ši·** whipping or destroying god, and **xaščéłčí·ˀ** the red god. [2] They sat erect but, when they endeavored to speak, they failed. They moved their eyes and head, but otherwise were unable to move or utter a sound.

---

[2] This would account for at least seven hashch-e, though there are six male and six female hashch-e in mask sets.

First-man then blew the following upon them: **'aciñlẍiš** zigzag lightning, **xaco·lγał** straight lightning, **xaǯiłgiš** flash lightning, **ńł-cą̨ẍó·l** rainray, **šábíẍó·l** sunray, **šáńdí·n** sunlight, **ná·ćí·lid** rainbow **ná·ćí·lid 'agodí** stubby rainbow, **šábíẍáǯiłči·'** reflected sunred, all of which formed their sinews, veins and arteries. Yet they were unable to move.

Next he blew white, blue, yellow, dark, pink winds (**ńłči**) into them. The cornbeetle (**'ańłťáni**) who lived inside of the darkness (**čaxałxe·ł**) owned **cáγádíńdíni** rock crystal, which he blew upon them for eyes, while the winds blown into them became their **bi·' sizį** (soul) 'standing within them.' These winds entered all parts of their bodies, then left them at the fingertips, and some[3] of them were good, others mean. They could now walk, stand, move, see and breathe. The cornbeetle now blew upon the rock crystal again, and his voice (**bi·né·'**) entered these hashch-e enabling them to give their wu-u-hu-call. Thus they received their voice from the cornbeetle. They were sanctified but **do· yáłtˣi'da** they never spoke, they could merely move about and see things.

It appears that **γé'i· naγâ·gi** 'sofaras the living ye-i are concerned' **če·h 'á·l'į·d** 'efforts were useless' when the assembled creators strove to make them speak. The buckskins were designated property for the future human (Navaho) race, while the jewels were carried away by the holy ones. (It is not clear what is meant. I presume the **ni·ƙéhé** fingernail face prints of jewels, mentioned in the early part of this paper, are meant). Therefore masked impersonators of these ye-i are admonished never to speak in their masks, owing to the original decision (reached after much effort) that the ye-i "**do· yáłtˣi'da** cannot speak."

Masks are marked off with rock crystal, and pollen is strewn

---

[3] Some refers to the hashch-e who became good because of a good or kind wind standing within them, and some were mean because a mean wind took possession of their bodies.

over this mark for the eyes and mouth, then cut out in imitation of what was done originally. A masked impersonator is believed to go blind, or to take sick and die, if he would venture to speak 'in the mask.' And because these holy people tried, in a holy way, to speak but failed, they are called **xaščé**, an inverted **čé·h xa·ʒí·'** he failed to speak. Therefore too, **čó bina·lγé** 'spruce is their wealth or possession' instead of the jewels, waterpots and clouds of the legends.

The talking god stands in the dawn and breathes there, which causes the dawn to appear in the east. In like manner, the calling god in the west, and the gods at the other cardinal points (**yi·' na·zį**) stand within the phenomena at those points and by their breath cause them to appear. All stand in **ƛos dilxił** dark cloud with the lower parts of their bodies, while the upper half is immersed in **nańse'** plants, and their chins in **t'ádídí·n** pollen. Therefore their prayersticks are half black, half blue, while the butt of the stick is punctured to receive the pollen. (It appears that these ritual regulations were established at that time).

They next discussed the character of their food. Talking god sang two songs 'with which' they ate **xayołká·ł b'xádídí·n** dawn's pollen and **šá b'xádídí·n** sunlight's pollen. During the meal first-man lined up the **na·lγéhé** goods (jewels) and the food in four rows along the north and south sides (of the hogan), while talking god sang and spoke and the goods also spoke and sang four times.[4] They were dressed in **ńƛiz** jewels, and when dressed in this manner they were all happy (and contented), and talking god sang (of this) again.

---

[4] There are, as a matter of course, song words which, even now, may be sung in the masks by performers. This is probably meant by having the ye-i and even the jewels 'sing and speak.' More than likely we have a reference here to the vigil or 'feeding of the masks' observed on the fourth night of a nine-night Night-way ceremonial.

Then talking god blew the white dawn toward the east, stood on it and entered (**biɫ ʼe·ldoh** it moved with him) into **sisna·ʒiñ** Blanca Peak. Calling god did likewise with skyblue and **ʼaxí·ka·d** moved into **co·ʒiɫ** Mt Taylor. Talking god repeated with evening twilight and entered into **do·ƙoʼosɫí·d** San Francisco Peak. Calling god repeated with darkness and entered **dibéñca·** La Plata range. (The notes on 'masks' for the assignment and birth of the gods at the cardinal points should be consulted here).

I find much confusion about the 'homes' of these gods. However, if one recalls Navaho fundamental concepts, especially of a multiplicity of talking and calling gods who are assigned, either in pairs as **ʼaɫké·ʼ naʼ·ʼaši·** *one follows the other*, or singly, without a companion, to homes at cardinal points, homes in sacred mountains and elsewhere, confusion is likely to disappear to a great extent. You abandon the idea that there is only one talking, one calling god, and accept them as they come, the one or the two: assigned to Blanca Peak or to San Francisco Peak.

If they are made to be the **bi·ʼ sizî·ni·** *in-standing-one* of such mountains, or the **bi·ʼ gistˣí·n** *in-lying-one* of these mountains or localities you accept that at its face value, just for what the terms mean. Your informant may not be able to explain these except to say that they are the soul or moving power of such mountains, whatever that may mean! They live there, with their families, as other mortals do. Mountains, rock cliffs and recesses are alive with them. The foreigner smiles, the Navaho knows better!

Therefore a sacrificial prayerstick is made (to the ye-i) and meal is strewn on the dancers, because the ye-i are supposed to appear from these homes in person (at the Nightway dance). The impersonator and the ye-i are (identified here and) conceived as one person.

The ye-i are conceived as **diγin dineʼé** holy people, who live in **kiní·nê·igai** white (streaked) house (Canon de Chelley). This is perhaps identified with **xayołká·ł be· xo·γan** home of dawn, and **naxo·coi be· xo·γan** home of evening twilight. (My notes are not too clear on this point). Wherever these two 'homes of dawn and evening twilight' may be, the ye-i supposedly have their homes. Other homes of the ye-i are also mentioned: **cé xaltˣá·l** *kicked-out rock* (?), **cé biní·ʼ** the *stone's center*, **cé níʼíči·ʼ** *red midrock*, **ƙíhiẓoʼó** (?) mountain. (The following was perhaps not carefully recorded in 1908). My notes read: **ƙos diłxił bixo·γango** *when their homes are dark cloud*, instead of **ƙos diłxił be· xo·γangó·** *along or in the homes of dark cloud.* The following are recorded: **ʼá·h bixo·γango** *their homes of mist*, **tˣó biyá·ž bixo·γango** *their homes of water's child*, and **tˣó ʼáłah náščí·n bixo·γango** *their homes of collected water.* Instrumental **be·** *of* and locative enclitic **-gó·** *along or in* seem to be required here, if we are to consider these as materials of the homes of the ye-i.

And yet, since no text in the vernacular is available, one can arrive at the sense by accepting, for example, **ʼá·h bixo·γango** *if their homes are mist*, or **ʼá·h be· xo·γangó·** *along their homes (made) of mist.* In either event the translation is unsatisfactory. A text in the vernacular alone could clarify the meaning which an informant wishes to convey. Let us be fair to native informants if they present their information in their own language. Other native informants are then in a position to check up on such statements, as I see it, and to interpret points of argument which are not brought out in free English translations through native interpreters.

These, as anybody who cares to learn about them knows, are not authoritative interpreters of ceremonial matters, but will readily substitute their personal interpretations on hieratic terms and matters in which they have no training. Interpreters are not trained in hieratic terminology much less are they initiated into Navaho ceremonialism as professional singers by the simple process of being employed as interpreters for an investigator. Let us not overlook such very simple facts in Navaho ceremonial researches. Much has been said and written on Navaho ceremonial subjects. But does the interpreter's version really convey the informant's mind? I hesitate to subscribe to this view. In matter of fact I have preferred texts in the vernacular, because I believe they give us a better checkup on divergent opinions which we may expect in a system that is liquid, to say the least.

The **céłčí·i·** red stone and **łico·í** yellow, were blown to the east by the nine-group: two pairs of **'ácé xastˣi·n** and **'ácé 'eszą́·n,** first-man and woman, by **'ácé 'aški·, 'ácé 'ațé·d,** first boy and girl, by **'ácé xazlį́·'** and **'aké·dę́·' xazlį́·'** first and second in origin, and by **'ácé xašké** first scolder or coyote. It appears that a decision was sought to let the appearance of yellow on the eastern horizon indicate health, growth, and all that is good. The appearance of the red stone color on the horizon would indicate **łó·d coh** smallpox, **dokos coh** big or whooping cough, **di·čin** hunger and all evil.

The nine-group interfered saying that they would have their own mind about this. But yellow is always good, red stone (**céłčí'i·**) always bad which seems to imply that disease is due to the witchery of the nine-group, and a red streaked horizon will portend this. A yellow horizon will portend health and prosperity.

The preceding account is assigned to **xóžǫ́·ǯí** Blessingway by **giši·ñ biγe'.** Also the songs of talking god, and the visits of the ye-i at the white house and other ye-i homes. (But the account on the whole is too vague for a good understanding of Blessingway rite. The nine-group especially are not associated with this rite, but with witchcraft).

Origin of Changing Woman. Two **bé·š diłxił no·lγíni·** *dark agate flints,* are seen floating in the skies. The **'ácé dahnálkǫ'i·** *first floating one,* is seen by the sun who calls it **bé·š**

diłxił šiγe' *my son dark flint.* This dark flint son is raised in the first floater in a supernatural way, and is dressed in wealth by the sun, who later lowers him down on the earth as **γé'i· coh** the *big terror* or ye-i. The **'aké·dę́·' dahnálkǫ'i·** *second floating one,* he also calls **bé·š diłxił ša'áłčíní** *my dark flint children.* These the sun tried to kill as he saw them floating in the agate following the first floater, but did not succeed. Therefore he called them **na·γé·' ne·zγání** *monster slayer* and **tˣó bážíščíní,** *born-for-water.* These two do not engage in killing beings on earth, but they seem to be prototypes of the two slayers that later cleansed the earth, (**'ái biƙehgo ye· 'aγą́,** *they direct the killing to be done*). The first floater seems to have been born to **są'ah na·γái** long life (woman), the second floater to **biƙeh xóžǫ́** happiness (woman). [5]

After **žó·ž diłxaší** the snapping vagina, had given birth to monstrous beings, and **γé'i· coh** big ye-i had been born in the skies and brought down on this earth, it so happened that first-man and woman heard the cry of a child four times at **čó·l'į́·'** Gobernador Knob. They picked it up and both called her *my daughter,* although she was the child of talking god and the dawn (**xayołká·ł**). It seems that the entire nine-group, mentioned before, found the girl and recognized her as their daughter. [6]

And they would address her **'eszą́· náλehé** *woman who time and again is transformed* and she would respond with **yá** *what* and come to them. Twelve days after her birth she had her **kina·sda',** **kina·ldá·h ńlį́** *first menstruation.* Therefore at present girls have their first menses when they are twelve years of age. Her first

[5] This section has reference to sky beings and properly belongs to starlore. In a manner however it appears to be introduced into the 'Origin of ye-i' to explain why monster slayer and born-for-water are numbered with ye-i and masks are made for them.

[6] This account of changing woman is very fragmentary and disagrees in several details with other more reliable sources. I have allowed it to stand because it leads up to the birth of the monster slayer and his brother on this earth. The prototypes of these slayers in the sky are non-related to them.

name was *changing woman.* But when **yołgai be· xadilyá** *she was dressed in white bead and other jewel clothes,* she received the name **yołgai ›eszą́·n** *white bead woman* ever after, and this accounts for the use of these two names in songs and prayers.[7]

At her puberty ceremony talking god sang the twelve hogan songs (mentioned elsewhere). All songs sung here were made holy and later added to Blessingway. Talking god finished with the 12-word Blessingway song (which is transcribed elsewhere in his **xa›nełnéhe·** Upward-reachingway legend).

After the ceremony all holy people left for their homes and the 9-person witch group alone remained. During the ceremony first-man and his associates had their own evil foods of corn and plants. To protect changing woman the holy ones provided her with corn and foods of her own, and these she was to use for the future human race. She had her own food of good quality, while first-man and associates ate evil red and mixed colored foods. She refused to touch these although first-man reminded her of the care that they had given her in her childhood. And when he pressed her for a reason she reminded them that they were not her parents (although they had not appraised her of this). He admitted that she was not their child and that they were neither sister nor brother to her. They ate in anger and apart from her, and finally left toward[8] the east, while changing woman journeyed to the west.

When they were about to leave they mentioned various evils, such as smallpox and violent diseases, which would kill people. In the west there was a house, an exact duplicate of the sun's house in the east. Here she found the two 'floating' women, **›ałké·› na·›aši·** *the two who travel one behind the other* of chang-

[7] Perhaps too it accounts for some confusion about the personality behind these two names.

[8] More properly towards the northeast which is commonly assigned to them as their home.

ing women. (The notes are reproduced here as written. Changing woman does seem to meet *long life and happiness* women in the west home. But these are not identical with the **'ałké'' na''aši'**).[9]

A note on **ʒiłe·ž** *mountain soil*, or **'aze''** *medicine*, used in **xó-žǫ·ʒí** Blessingway ceremonies. Soil from the following mountains is employed: Blanca Peak, Mt Taylor, San Francisco Peak, La Plata range, from **ʒił ná'o·diłi·** Huerfano, **čô·l'į·'** Gobernador Knob, **'ałinastání** the Crown Point near Pueblo Bonito, **čóšgai** Chuska Peak, **cisna·tˣe·l** wide mesa, east of Huerfano. This soil is wrapped in five small bags, made of pieces of unwounded buckskin. The usual jewels of all colors, and **xadaxoniγe'** mirage stones, white, blue, yellow and dark are added. Also **'ąh nano·gá·d** pollens shaken from live birds. The whole is then placed into a large piece of unwounded buckskin and wrapped with buckskin thongs. During any Blessingway ceremony this pouch must be held in the hand by the singer. The small soil bags are imbedded in corn pollen and rock crystal added before the wrapping is done. (There is a **do''i·γa·ž** no-sleep[10] to **'ańłtáni·** corn beetle, in thanksgiving for food crops). **teščí''** specular iron ore (may be employed for the pouch).

---

[9] Again this has reference to star people of the 'second' floater.

[10] This reference to the no-sleep ceremony of the fourth night of Nightway and its direction to the corn-beetle justifies informant's note on the mountain soil pouch. He knew that any native will understand that any reference to mountain soil, to a no-sleep ceremony can only mean a Blessingway ceremony. If in Nightway the feeding of the masks is a no-sleep ceremony of the fourth night it means that most songs are chosen from Blessingway without rattle and drum. These must be silent, but the singer in the lead holds the mountain soil pouch in his hand while these songs are sung.

Chapter Two

Making and Trimmings of Masks

In **ƛé·ʒí** Nightway the following masks appear (not necessarily in the order here given):

1. **xaščéltˣiʾí** talking god;
2. **xaščéʾo·γa·n** calling god;
3. **xaščé bᵃkąʾ** male gods, 6 in number;
4. **xaščé baʾá·d** female gods, 6 in number;
5. **xaščéšžiní** black god;
6. **na·γé·ʾ ne·zγání** monster slayer;
7. **tˣó báʒíščíní** born-for-water;
8. **xaščʾéłbáhí** or **tˣó neinili·** gray god or water sprinkler;
9. **γą́· ʾaskidi·** hump back;
10. **zaxado·lžahí** fringed mouth;
11. **xaščéłčí·ʾ** red god;
12. **xá·dači·ši·** destroyer or whipping god;
13. **xaščé ʾidí·łćǫ·s** whistling god;
14. **xaščé ʾołtohí** shooting god;

This list taken in 1908 includes all masks appearing in Nightway even today. Not much could be learned of no. 13 and which mask is used to impersonate him. The same informant of 1908 stated that in **xaščé cohe·** Big Godway the masked **xaščé coh** big god represents **bᵃγʷo· ʾaxínásgai** *one with the double row of white teeth.* I did not however find this statement repeated in my text of this chantway.

In **mąʾi·ʒí** Coyoteway nos. 1 and 10 are featured inside the hogan. A different view is expressed later.

Masks are mentioned for these branches of Nightway: **tˣáłƛá·h-ʒí** water bottom branch; **cinćá· xatˣá·l** ceremonial 'away from' the tree; **tˣó ná·ʒí** (probably from **tˣó wóna·ńʒí**) across water branch. Also for **ʼaćoseˑ** Downway and for **mąʼiˑǯí** Coyoteway.

After these remarks about masks in general our informant tells something about the birth of the **γéˑʼiˑ** and probably voiced opinions expressed by his brother **xastˣiˑn yáží** Small Man of the Ganado, Arizona, area. In the preceding chapter this informant seemed to be concerned more about the **niˑƙéhé** face prints (or masks) of the **γéˑʼiˑ** than with their personalities. In the following abstract he seems to describe the origin of beings whom the Navaho call **γéˑʼiˑ**. As said before the account was not taken in the vernacular and represents an interpreter's translation in note form.

The **γéˑʼiˑ** originated after the emergence from the lower worlds. At the **xaǯíˑnái** emergence place, four farms extended out from it at the cardinal points in this fashion:

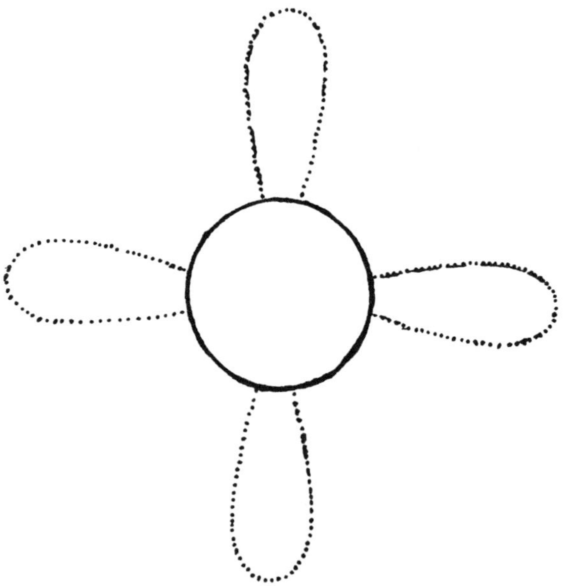

Four homes of corn were found one at each cardinal point. In the east there was **na·dą̨·łgai be· xo·γan** a home of white corn where **xayołká·ł xastˣi·n** dawn man and **xayołká·ł ›eszą̨·** dawn woman gave birth to their son **xaščéłtˣi›í** (1) talking god.

In **na·dą̨·łcoi be· xo·γan** the home of yellow corn of the west **naxo·coi xastˣi·n** evening twilight man and **naxo·coi ›eszą̨·** evening twilight woman gave birth to **xaščé›o·γa·n** (2) calling god and to **xá·da›či·si·** (12) the destroyer or whipping god.

In **tˣádídį·›** **be· xo·γan** the pollen home of the south **naxode·-ƛi·ž xastˣi·n** and **›eszą̨·** horizontal blue man and woman gave birth to **xaščé ba›á·d** female gods.[11]

In the **nańse›** **be· xo·γan** home of vegetation of the north **čaxałxe·ł xastˣi·n** and **›eszą̨·** darkness man and woman produce **tˣádídį· ›aški·** pollen boy and **›ańłťáni· ›aťé·d** corn beetle girl.[12]

When the various **ńłči** winds, white, yellow, blue and black entered the bodies of talking god (east), male (west), and female gods (south), these failed to speak, **čé·h xa·zí·›** they tried but failed to utter words, or **čé·h dayí·ł›į·d** they (the winds) failed in their effort. The inverted form **xaščé·h,** instead of **čé·h xa·zí·›** is generally accepted to connote this effort 'to make them speak' and suggests 'speechless' for Navaho **xaščé·h** or **xaščé.**

The corn beetle received its voice in the corn home of the east and gave the 'speechless ones' what voice **bi·né·›** they have. Therefore they have calls: in the east wu-u-u-hu; in the west hawo·, hawo·›, in the south wu-u-wu·; in the north corn beetle's lo-lo-looo. No particular meaning is attached to these calls. They equate with the corn beetle's **loool-call** and, informant holds,

---

[11] This would include six female gods just as those of the west include six male gods of whom calling god is the leader in dance groups. Informant mentions only one representative of the male and female groups.

[12] These two, pollen boy and corn beetle girl are not numbered among the γé·›i·, but corn beetle at least has a call of its own and, as said in the following, it gives the γé›i· what little 'voice' they have.

that the corn beetle gave the ye-i of the other cardinal points 'what voice they have.'[13]

In substance the preceding account appears to concern itself with Nightway **'acáłe·h ćósí** the 'slim' first dancers. These are inducted, as we shall see later, by talking god (1) who does not dance. Calling god (2) leads the first dancers proper and also the socalled 'slim' first dancers in dance and song. As there are only male and female dancers in the final exhibitions informant emphasizes these ye-i more than others that do not appear as dancers. But, whether dancers or not, the principle holds, that none of the ye-i 'speak.' They may have their calls, but that is either **'ání** it calls, or **bi·né·'** their voice, not a **yát'i'** speech! The corn beetle is typical for its call, not for its speech.

A number of informants when questioned seemed to prefer to take the **γé·'i·** for granted without entering into their origin as well as that of their masks which they left behind for use by the Navaho. They appear more concerned about assigning them to specific localities such as **céní·'í** midrock, **céní'íči·'** red midrock, and to **kiní·' nêigai** white streak house or the white house of Canyon de Chelley. Who made the assignment is not stated except that corn beetle gave them their provisions and even their voices.

While this may be interpreted to imply that they were to subsist on corn products no such specific statement was made by any informant. However before the ye-i people left for the homes to which they were assigned 'they took **ni·ƙéhé** face prints of themselves in white bead, turquoise, abalone, and jet, but directed that humans should reproduce them in buckskin.'

---

[13] Apparently informant scores his point that corn beetle, in a class by himself, is responsible for ye-i calls similar to his own. We need not insist too much on discovering why corn beetle girl had to go to the corn home in the east to get her 'voice' and then be able to supply the ye-i with 'what voice' they have. The north is icy and frigid and corn beetle loves corn raising climes! This, of course, is my own not a suggestion made by native informants.

Therefore the buckskin masks of today represent their (real) faces and are painted white, blue, red or black in imitation of the original jewel face prints. And, too, because the γé·ˀi· group has voice or call, but not speech-utterance, all impersonators of them are prewarned not 'to speak' into the masks.

Masks are either head or face masks made of unwounded buckskin. The mask of talking god employs **bį̄h bᵃkąˀí** male deer, or buckskin for the face, **bį̄h baˀá·di** doeskin, for the back of the head, and the sinew of both is employed to sew the two halves together. For the eyes of all masks and the mouths pollen is strewn, the eye and mouth holes are marked with **cáγádíńdíní** rock crystal, then punctured with an arrowhead or a knife. The face colors are mineral colors: **λe·š** native almogen furnishes white, **(cé) be· di·lχiš,** a soft blue ocher, mixed with white furnishes the blue, **łe·ǯin** (perhaps **łe·łižin**) a black ocher furnishes black, especially for the eyes. The butt end of **ˀade·ˀ** a gourd, furnishes the mouth pieces wherever these are required and a fluff of **mąˀi· do·χiži** kit fox, encircles it. In paintings of masks this fluff is shown in white.

The eyes and mouth of talking god (1) are **biná·ˀ bizé· ˀaxí·sinil** eyes and mouth lie together, that is, two open squares are fitted into each other as shown on mask No. 1.

The fluff around the mouth indicates a gourd tip and kit-fox hair. The face of the mask is white and the eye and mouth squares are drawn on the mask in black. From the mouth upward a corn plant is also drawn in black, showing five leaves and two ears of corn, with the corn tassel near the forehead. The yellow and white borders at the bottom of the mask flap represent the evening twilight and dawn, and are shown on all masks. Talking god should wear **čó yi·lbá·ˀ** a spruce collar. Along the seam of the mask **łį́·γa·ˀ** hair of a horse's mane, is added to represent **ńłcą́ na·ǯi·n,** drooping rain. Some **ˀace·ˀ łagai** white eagle tail feathers, (some say twelve) should be secured to the top of the mask (at least in γʷóneʼé xatʼáʼl the inside or 'just visiting' ceremonial.) At their base two tufts of né·šʒ̨a·γa·ʼ fluffy owl feathers are stuck. At the tips of the eagle feathers ʼaćos łagai white downs are set. On the tips of the extreme downs two bluebirds rest facing each other, the dóli· bᵃką̇ʼí or male bluebird, resting on the right side of the mask, the dóli· baʼá·dí or female bluebird, on the mask's left side. These bird decorations were probably added in the legends, in practice bluebird feathers are more feasible, or may be omitted. Talking god always leads masked impersonators, and holds a gourd in his right, a fawn bag with pollen or meal in his left hand. On his forehead he wears an olivella or white bead shell from which two bį̨h bice·ʼ deer tails dangle, probably to indicate his control of game.

Although xaščéʼo·γa·n calling god, (2) frequently accompanies talking god, he is not associated with him in certain masked groups, as when the talking god leads the meal sprinklers to invite singers to attend the closing celebrations. His is a blue head mask, with the eagle feathers, downs, bluebird, horsehair and owl fluffs exactly like those of the talking god mask. The eyes, the common triangles of masks, the mouth the common square. These are punctured and the outlines painted black. He wears the spruce collar, a buckskin, beads, nice moccasins and pants.

The male gods (3) wear a blue head mask, the seam of which shows the drooping rain in black horsehair. Two ʼace·ʼ white eagle tail feathers, extend on the right side of the mask, tipped with the ʼaćos łagai white downs, and the usual owl feathers at their base. Male gods wear a spruce collar. A tʼažićos, turkey down, forms the peak of the mask, and this is crowned by ʼaćos łagai, the common white down headplume. A bluebird rests at the base of the turkey and eagle plumes. The eyes are the common triangular type, the mouth is provided with a gourd mouthpiece fluffed with kit fox hair.

The female (4) gods require a blue face mask with the usual triangular eyes, a plain square mouth without beard or mustache, and a ladder-like figure extending over the mouth to represent **bíčįh** its nose. The neck flaps expose the evening twilight and dawn bands, and indicate **ńłcą́ na·ʒi·n** the drooping rain. No collar is required. The forehead circle also indicates a band of horsehair for the drooping rain. The headplume consists of a turkey down and an eagle down (**tˣaži·ċos** and **'aċos łagai**), at the base of which rests **cídi·łcoi** a yellow bird or canary. At the joint where these downs are inserted a lump of **ƛe·š za·ńił** or white ocher medicine, is placed for future use.

Distinctive of this mask are also the white **'aʒa·'**, ear flaps on both sides of its face. The edges of these flaps are slightly cut in to represent the **'óxo·ʒánígí·** or openings, through which the **ńłči xoł xalni'ígí·** informing winds, advise them. The extending thongs over these white flaps are the **ʒa·' biẍó·l** ear's cord, which serve to tie the mask on the back of the head. The blue pendants at the lower extremities of these thongs are the **ʒa·ẍó·ł** ear cords, or turquoise ear pendants. Men usually dress as females, but women too do not hesitate to act as female-god impersonators, especially in public exhibitions.

The **xaščéłbái** or gray god (8) is the clown of the group. He is also known as **tˣó neinili·** water carrier or sprinkler, and messengers are frequently dispatched to him in legends to request the use of his pots and control of sacred waters. His mask is a blue head mask, with the horsehair at the seams, and two eagle feathers stuck in the right side and owl feathers at their base. The two eagle feathers are tipped with downy feathers as usual. The base or neck of the mask is concealed by a spruce collar. In his right **mą'i· do·ẍiž yołtˣé·ł** he holds a kit fox, which **yiłmąs** he twirls as he walks along. At his wrists **tˣaži·γa·'** turkey fluff, and **lašdǿ·n** a red and blue band are attached, and in his left hand he holds **čǿ binesťą'** spruce bundles with cones at their tips. A **yo·' nó·mazi· nážahí bąsitˣą́** silver bead necklace with crescent pendant, is seen hanging under his right armpit. A **lašdǿ·n** or colored (blue, green, red) ribbon band is slung from his right shoulder to his left hip, where a bundle of turkey down is tied to the ribbons together with two white eagle tail feathers.

A white **sis dolγéli** or knotted sash (?) forms his **ƛa·kał** or kilt, in the rear of which **mą'iłcoi,** yellow fox is **sis dahdétˣį́h gǿne'** stuck into the folds of his belt. The legs like body and arms are white, but he wears blue stockings held with red **ʒ̨ánéží** garters, and **bike·'** his moccasins. In the right legging or stocking a white eagle (tail) feather is stuck with branches of spruce, in the left legging only spruce branches are seen. Gray god always makes up the rear in the group of dancers, regardless of their number. By his foolish pranks he adds much to the entertainment of visitors.

Depending upon the branch of a Nightway ceremonial to be celebrated the head mask of fringed mouth (10) will show the right half of its face red or yellow. The left half is always blue. We have therefore: **céní·ʒ̨í zaxadolžahá biní·' łičí·'** midrock branch fringed mouth whose face is red, and **tˣáłƛá·hʒ̨í zaxadolžahá biní·' łicoi** water bottom branch fringed mouth whose face is yellow. Excepting for this distinction there are no differences in the two masks. The triangular eyes and the round (gourd) mouth are 'fringed' with white color. A center line in black with three white cross lines at four points separates the two colored halves of the face, forehead to chin, and probably suggests 'darkness' of the north. Two **mą'i do·ƛiži·** kitfox skins are employed as **yi·lbá·'** collars, and their heads may be crossed on the front with tails dangling down the back, or the heads may be crossed on the left shoulder and tails on the right.

These masks are provided with ears, blue for the left ears, red and yellow for the right side as the mask requires. Blue turquoise (**ʒa·Xó·ł**) pendants are attached to the ears. A thin black fuzz is added around the outer edge of the mask to indicate its **bici·ʼ** hair.

A **báššini· ċa·ʼ** jet basket is set upon the mask, but this requirement of the legends is now met by cutting the bottom out of any native basket (**ċa·ʼ**) which then becomes part of the singer's pouch. A cone shaped peak made of **łį·γa·ʼ** horsehair, supported by sticks, is set into the basket. The tip of this **tˣá·ʼaċos** forehead plume, (or three-down) is decorated with three **ʼaċos łagai** white downs, set up erect, but one leaning to the mask's left, all of which are wrapped with cotton cord and secured to the tip. A number of **ʼace·łčí·ʼ** red tail or flicker feathers, are set up at the base of the cone within the basket, and the basket with its cone and decorations is called **tˣá· ʼastˣá·n** 'set on the forehead'. The masks are decorated anew in this manner for each performance.

The headmask of **γą́· ʼasǩidi·** hump back, (9) also called **ná· ʼasǩidi·** hump eye, has a blue face, plain triangular eyes, a fluffed (gourd) mouth, blue ears (**biʒa·ʼ**), turquoise pendants (**ʒa·Xó·ł**) surmounted by two **céłčíʼi·** red stones. Two **mąʼiłcoi** yellow foxes, are employed for the **yi·łbá·ʼ** collar, heads crossed at center. The head cover of the mask is a cutout rim of a basket marked with **ʼacińłXiš** zigzag lightning lines on the outside of the basket. Two **bide·ʼ** horns, made of twisted sheep or goat skin, painted blue with zigzag lightning lines on their fronts, are set into the basket and curved out in opposite directions. At the horn tips the **ʼaċos łagai** or white downs are secured with cotton cord (**Xózó·ł**). Inside of the basket a number of **ʼace·łčí·ʼ** red flicker (tail) feathers and **ʼace·ʼ łižin** black tail feathers, are set upright. This head cover too is called **tˣá· ʼastˣą́·n** 'placed on the forehead.' The hair on the mask are turned in.

In addition the **xe·ł** burden or hump, must be made anew for every performance. A stuffed sheep pelt is employed and decorated on the outer surface in rainbow colors (white, blue, white, red, white). Into this hump five **'ace·łgai** white tail feathers, and five **'ace·łčí·'** red tail feathers are stuck. Two cords representing **šá biXó·l** sunrays, are added, with which the performer ties the burden to his back. He walks with a cane in a stooped position and occasionally gives his mournful call **'í·yahą̂·n.**

The head mask of **xaščéšžini** (5) is altogether black. The hair surrounding the mask are profusely turned out for 'drooping rain.' Eye and mouth holes are punctured and **yo·' dižo·lí** olivella shells, are secured there. A white spot of **λe·š** white clay, is painted on the forehead, and is later employed as **za·ńił** medicine food. A white **'ac̓os coh** eagle down, is added to the right side of the mask, and two yellow fox skins are employed as collars.

The black god is the god of fire. Hence his **xono·γé·ł** or fire bundle, is usually depicted with him. It consists of **'aží·h** bark, **cá'ászi' ńtˣe·lí be'esXǫ́** tied with wide yucca thongs (shown at left side of mask drawing). It is also related that, in the lower worlds, he rubbed his body and prepared a meal of these cuticles. Hence four **náneska·di·** or slap cakes are strung on **cá·ászi'** a yucca blade (shown on lower right) and are called 'his cakes'. These too are sought by singers, **za·ńił 'ída·l'į́,** medicine foods are made of them.

The head masks of **na·γé·' ne·zγání** monster slayer (6) and of **tˣó bážíščíní** born-for-water (7) are decorated with **'ac̓os coh** large eagle down, on the right side of the masks, and both show the profuse horsehair around the edges. Both add the white clay (**λe·š**) on the forehead (for **za·ńił** medicine food). A **yołgai** white bead, is placed beside the white clay on monster slayer's mask, a turquoise (**do·Xiži**) on born-for-water's mask. Monster slayer employs a kit-fox collar, born-for-water a yellow fox collar. The **bibé·ž** knife of monster slayer is made of **bé·š diłxił** dark flint, his **bᵃγáł** or rattle of **desci·n** pinyon. The knife of born-for-water is made of blue flint, his rattle of **gad** cedar. (These are shown below the two masks).

The mask of monster slayer is black with squares punctured for eyes, a round hole for the mouth, but an olivella shell is fastened over the eye and mouth openings. Distinctive are five four-angled zigzag lightnings drawn in white on the right (?) cheek of this mask. The bow symbol shown at the upper left of the mask denotes that **ˀałtˣí·n ye· xadíłê·go sizį** 'he stands clothed in bows.' Therefore the impersonator must draw the bow symbol on his legs, thigh, arms, shoulders and back.

The face of the mask of born-for-water has a red background on which the queue (hair bundle) symbol is drawn. The first symbol on the right side of the chin must show the opening directed to the mask's mouth, all others have the symbol closed. Eyes and mouth are square openings with an olivella shell above them. The eyes and mouth are set on a black panel slightly rounded below the mouth and bordered white all around. The impersonator must decorate his body with **ci·γé·ł ye· xadíłê·go sizį** the queue symbol in which he stands clothed. This must be left open as shown in the upper left hand corner above the mask.

A face mask of **xašč̓éłčí·ˀ** red god (11) is used whenever the 9-night ceremonial is observed inside the hogan **t̓ó· na·ʒ̨éhégo xatˣá·l** (when ceremonial is merely by visiting) or **γʷóneˀé xatˣá·l** inside kind of ceremonial, but not in the **na·ˀakai** 'they repeatedly come in' that is, the public masked dance. The face is red, with a black panel bordered white like that of born-for-water. The eyes are triangular, mouth square. The upper edge shows the regular horsehair trimming, and a turkey feather and **ˀac̓os łagai** white down, secured to the center of the mask and the white clay spot at their base.

The white ear flaps on either side are fringed at the edges 'for information' as already mentioned for the female-god face masks.

Thongs are provided to allow the operator to secure the mask to the head. The lower edges under the evening twilight and dawn lines are usually **be· naščą̨·ˀ** designed or decorated in blue, yellow, white. Drooping rain streaks are shown in black through the dawn and evening twilight, as on most masks.

The **xá·da·či·ši** whipping or destroyer god (12) has a blue head mask with the common triangular eyes and plain square mouth, but a nose in white (ladder-shaped) is set over the mouth between the eyes. The horsehair fringe is seen around the whole seam of the two halves. The mask is decorated with **ˀaćos łagai** white plume on the right side, and with a turkey feather and white plume on the top of the mask. The small white hoops shown below the mask indicate that **bą̨s ye· xadíté** hoops are his clothes. Accordingly the impersonator should draw these on his body. The two yucca whips (**cá·ászi· beˀecˣis**) shown below the hoops, indicate that this god makes free use of these leashes: (Red god also whips). The prayerstick offering made to this god is placed near a solitary yucca plant. This mask too is not used at the **na·ˀakai** or public dance, but in **na·ǯéhégo xatˣá·l** inside ceremonial only.

He (**giši·ň biγeˀ**) adds that the horse's mane furnishes the fringes on the (seam) tops of all masks. The masks must be cut, sewed and painted at the vigil (fourth) night of a Nightway ceremonial. Two boys and two girls sprinkle water and pollen from baskets on the masks. (The idea is that the boys and girls are virgins, untouched as yet, by women or men). A feast of native foods is given (or fed) to the masks and placed on fine blankets, and eaten by those present. This dedication makes the masks the **ǯiš** or pouch of this chantway.

Speaking 'in' the mask causes cough, sores on dancer, provokes smallpox and stomach troubles. Therefore the dancers are prewarned. Persons that limped or had crooked joints were excluded from wearing masks. During the performance the singer always sings **xóžǫ·ʒí** Blessingway songs, and white and yellow meal with pollen are strewn on the dancers. After removing the mask the wearer should blow on the mask 'to drive the evil away.' Talking god and Calling god always favor benevolence and planned the origin of changing woman and Blessingway.

The preceding notes are based on interpretations by **giši·ň biγeʾ** in 1908. Supplementary notes are found in **ƛé·ʒí** notes on masks by **ci·ščili· ćósí,** the late Slim Curly of Crystal, N. M. (1934).

All male masks are head masks, female masks are face masks. (This statement is general only for **γéʾi· bᵃkąʾ** and **γéʾi· baʾá·d** male and female ye-i impersonator masks, not for other head and face masks). This informant cannot advance a good reason for this divergence of opinion. The taboo on speaking while wearing a mask, however, applies to both male and female masks. Important masks are those of talking god, calling god, monster slayer, born-for-water, and fringed mouth, all of which should be made of **ʾabań do·ƙa·ƙehi·** unwounded buckskin. If the supply of the latter is insufficient for all masks of a set, these five should be made first, for the others ordinary buckskin may be employed.

The hide is folded in the center and laid down flat so that the fore or head end can always be kept in mind. The thumb is set as a pivot where the mask's mouth is to be, and a circle is drawn around with the middle finger. Attention is paid to certain widths. Thus, the width of four fingers should be left on each side of the mouth and a little better than the width of five fingers below the mouth. With the thumb still resting on the mouth a small span with the index and middle fingers mark the points for the eyes, above which again the width of five fingers is left. The mask is then cut out and the folded portion in the center is cut in two. At the center points where the right and left seams will meet the two halves are sewed together and downy feather tips of **ʾayá·š**

diłxił, dark small birds and **dǒli·** bluebird, are crossed here and sewed in.

Formerly the rule obtained that the bone awl used in sewing the right half of the mask should be taken from the right foreleg of a deer, the awl for the left half from the left foreleg of the deer. Likewise the sinew for the right half had to be taken from the right tender loin, the sinew of the left half from the left side of a deer. Today the least requirement is that part of the two halves should be sewed with unwounded buckskin (sinew or) thongs. Tufts of bluebird down are sewed in with the right half seam, tufts of yellow warbler or canary with the left half seam. The back of the mask is daubed a pure white clay, the face blue, eyes and mouth black.

The eyes and mouth are cut out circular, but a triangular mark is fitted around the eyes, a square one around the mouth. Across the chin a black streak is drawn to represent darkness, below this a yellow one for evening twilight. On both sides down over the evening twilight two pairs of black lines are drawn to represent rainfall. (Drooping rain of the preceding informant).

When in actual use at a dance tufts of horsehair are attached to the seam to represent the hair of the head, but are detached immediately after the conclusion of the ceremonial. Of the six male and six female masks, the leader and end masks only are marked for recognition. The male and female leaders are marked by a turquoise, the end masks by a horsehair or a colored string. All other masks of this group carry an abalone shell.

Some masks carry special decorations. Thus talking god's mask (1) is painted white on both sides. The eyes and mouth are cut circular, but a square is set over a square around them. A cornstalk rises from the mouth up between the eyes with three leaves to the left, two to right of the stalk, two ears of corn, one on the center left leaf, the other on the lower right leaf. Chin

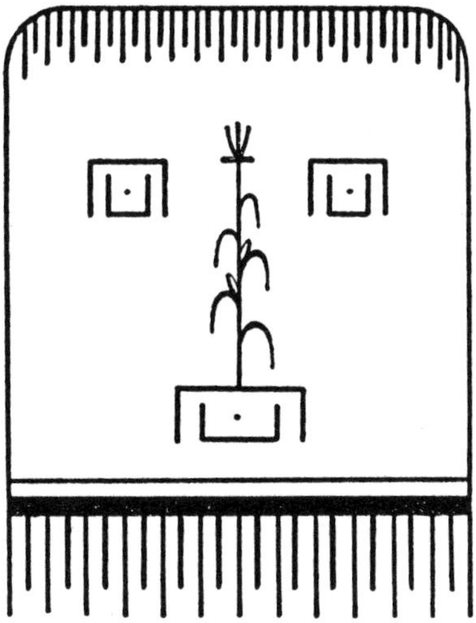

streaks and mane hair are found here also. (Originally the ye-i used **cébąh** **'aγa''ígí'** rock moss, but ordered that the mane of a horse (after its introduction) was to be used instead by earth people).

Charred weeds and collected tallows are employed for the black mask (6) of monster slayer, but the darkness streak is drawn with **łe'ǯin** coal, or black ocher. The eyes are cut round, but instead of the triangular mark around the eyes and the square around the mouth, a **yo''** **diǯo'lí,** olivella shell, is tied over eyes and mouth. Four **nanaxo'γazí** zigzag lines are drawn on the left side of the face to represent **gą'γaxašǯé''** the shoulder straps of monster slayer.

The back and face of **t'ó** **báǯíščíní** born-for-water (7) is red. Again olivella shells are attached over eyes and mouth. Between his eyes a solid triangle in black is set to represent 'his real looks.' No set number of **ci'γé'ł** hair bundles or queues are required on the face and back of the head, but the extreme lower right

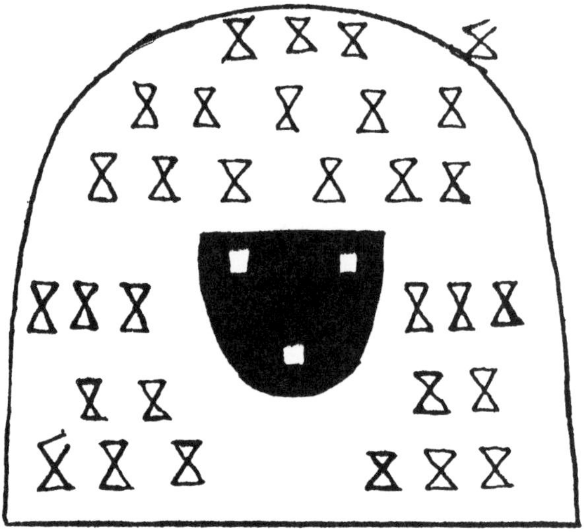

queue of the face and the queue in the extreme upper left corner of the back of mask are left open, all others closed.

Fringed mouth mask (10) is white on its back, the right half of its face is red, the left half blue. The right eye is a half crescent, the left eye is made 'fuzzy' with white marks around the black circle and the mouth is treated likewise. (Or rather, these fuzzy and crescent shaped marks are set over the cuts for the eyes and mouth). The oblong square between the eyes represents his nose.

A basket from which the bottom has been cut out is set on top of the mask when in use. Over this a **tˣá·ʼaċosi** head or forehead plume made of **kį·ʼ** sumac is secured with downy feathers attached to the tip. The basket rim is trimmed with **ťáya·łčí·ʼ bice·ʼ** flicker tail feathers, stuck in as head trimmings. The performer also carries a bow and rattle.

γą̂·ʼaskidi· hump back mask (9), rear white, face blue, eyes set in black triangles, mouth in a black square. He wears the basket head dress similar to fringed mouth, but instead of the triangular head plume horns are provided with tips turned out.

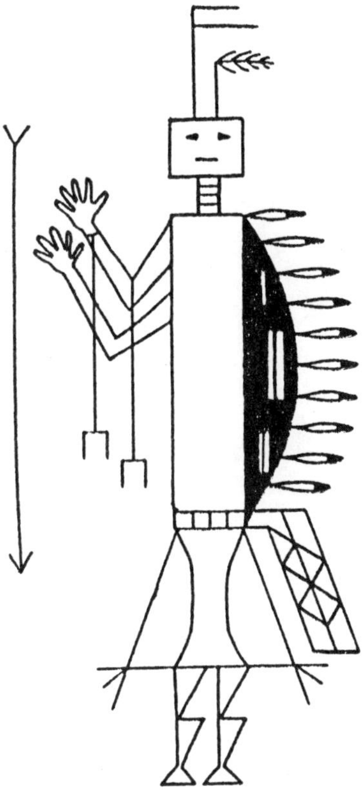

The lower part of the horns are black, the upper part blue, and the tips mounted with downy feathers. He carries a cane which he uses in the performance with his call. His hump is made of an oblong hoop spanned by a stave. A sheep pelt is drawn over this, allowed to dry and then daubed black. The white spots which are dotted here and there on this hump seem to have no special significance.

The black god (**xaščéšžini**) mask (5) is entirely black. The cuts for eyes and mouth are encircled by a white ring. A straight white line runs from his mouth between the eyes and is surmount-

ed by the crescent, **šáyi·tˣą̨** the new moon. On his left cheek **dilγéhé** Pleiades are drawn, but no special reason is assigned to this, although informant omits Pleiades in his (sand) paintings of Black god. In performances this god carries **kǫno·γé·ł** firebrand in his left hand, **náneska·dí** patted breads (slap cakes) in his right.

xaščéłčí·', red god mask (11) is all red, but only a face mask, for which informant assigns no reason. On eyes and mouth olivella shells are attached. Between his eyes the solid triangle of born-for-water is also added.

Calling god (2) is the leading mask of the six first dancers. He is followed by a female, after which two pairs of male and female dancers alternate. Talking god (1) leads and water sprinkler (8) brings up the end of this group of first dancers.[14]

Ordinarily the fringed mouth (10), hump back (9), hadach-ishi (12), black god (5), and red god (11) are considered special features and do not appear excepting by special request. The mask of hadach-ishi (12) is not described.[15]

xaščédódí (8) is so called from the call **dód dód** given by him as a clown.[16] This god is identical with **xaščéłbái** (8) gray god and with **tˣó neinili·** (8) water sprinkler. As gray god he is the clown of the dancing groups on the closing night. As water sprinkler he performs with **na·γé·ʼ ne·zγáń** monster slayer (6), **tˣó báǰíščíní** born-for-water (7), and **xaščéʼołťohí** shooting god (14), inside the hogan and is also entitled to a prayerstick. As **xaščédódí** (8) he performs on the initial nights of the ceremonial when unraveling is to be done. The masked performers are then **xaščéltˣiʼí** talking (1), a **xaščé baʼá·d** female god (4) or some other **xaščé** god, and **xaščédódí** (8). In the **ʼi·ká·h łání** many sandpaintings, **xaščédódí** (8) follows the six male (3) and six female **xaščé** (4) of that painting and he also figures in the deposit of prayersticks. At γé·ʼi·ʼaš, 'the ye-i enter or visit the neighborhood,' he is again **xaščéłbáhí** gray god or **tˣó neinili·** water sprinkler (8).

γé·ʼi·ʼaš, visiting (masked) performers. This is done on the morning of the second last day of the ceremonial. When the visionary made the set of masks for his brother and had performed the **do·ʼi·γa·ž** no-sleep for them, some attendants masked themselves with them and visited the people in the neighborhood. The masks

[14] While this is true of the ʼacáłeh čósí slim first dancers no. 8 does not appear in ʼacáłeh proper as I have pointed out later on.

[15] This too is discussed later.

[16] The dódí hashch-e performs over the patient with the small hoops on the first night of Nightway. In doing so he gives his *dod, dod* call.

were admired by the people who gave them pollens as an offering. Today pollens and foods are given to the visiting ye-i. The singer and his helpers keep the pollen brought in, but the foods are distributed at the meal for the public.

Restrictions, **(bićáde·táníɡí·)**.--*Eating*.-- At the close of the ceremonial the patient is enjoined not to eat the **ʼabid,** paunch, **ʼazid** liver, **ǯéi díšǯo·líɡí·** heart proper, and **dadiǯo·líɡí· tá·ałco** anything that is round, because these are similar in shape to the mask (**ǯiš**).

Wearing Masks. A person who is a member of a dancing group and has had Nightway performed over him, is subsequently forbidden to wear a mask of the set belonging to the performing singer. Should he nonetheless desire to use the set, he is required to tie a bead to 'his' mask that is, to the mask which he usually wears as a dancer in his team or group. This implies that one person is always the leader of his dancing group and wears the leading mask, say the male mask, the others follow in order and never change positions, either male or female. Speaking 'in the masks' is forbiden, presumably on the grounds that, as impersonator of the **xaščé** the masked dancer cannot speak. **xaščé·h** is said to be derived from **čé·h xa·ʒí·ʼ** he tried but failed to speak.

Feeding the Masks. The foods are lined up in the hogan as sketched on p. 51.

Any other foods as vegetables, meat, corn, even canned goods, coffee and other drinks may be added. Pollen is offered sunwise to the foods lined up before the masks. The **ńʼdi·ʼá biγi·n** songs of the uprights are sung after which all present feast on these foods. This should be done on the night of **do·ʼi·γa·ž,** no-sleep, when the **xóžǫ·ʒí** Blessingway or, as it is properly called: **ǯiš bicą· ʼálné·hgi,** 'when the food of the masks is made' is performed. Our informant however observes that, at present, foods are rarely brought inside. Nonetheless the songs must be sung.

Chapter Three

Navaho Head and Face Masks.

The student of Navaho religious life soon discovers a variety of ceremonials and a resultant variety of singers who conduct these ceremonials. He also learns that some ceremonials appear to be in a major class, others in a minor or less important class, if viewed by the notoriety given them and the attendance which they attract.

It is perhaps well, however, to recall that notoriety and large attendances are not a true criterion for native evaluations of their ceremonials. One soon discovers on this score that a small figurine ceremony is of importance to a native though few of the neighbors may attend. In matter of fact it may settle his troubles and prove economic in the end, whereas a ceremonial of longer duration may prove disastrous financially.

Comparing a morning's excerpt ceremony of reproducing a given figurine with a **biǯį́** or one-night closing ceremonial, the latter lasts longer than the former and may draw a larger attendance of neighbors. But compared with a war dance the latter will usually extend over three nights and draw visitors even outside the immediate neighborhood. The reason is that more publicity is given to it and the girls' dance connected with it, and the moving from one place to another is a distinctive public feature.

As for outsiders few will care to camp on the trail of moving natives for three days, but will prefer to attend the last or closing night. They come home with the idea, and express it, that they have seen and even participated in a Navaho war dance. In matter of fact they have attended the last of three performances two of which have taken place elsewhere on the two preceding nights and afternoon, albeit in an abbreviated form.

Larger ceremonials of nine-nights' duration are less frequent than those of the preceding types mentioned. Mountain-topway may be either a five- or a nine-night ceremonial with or without the corral dance. If the dance is dispensed with it is obvious that few people will attend the close of the ceremonial, whereas corral dances always attract a large attendance.

In Nightway too the patient has the choice of **ťő· na·ẑéhégő· xatˣá·l** just visiting sing, meaning that **γé›i·** or masked impersonators will not hold the **na›akai** *groups going here and there* or dance of the ye-i. Or he may arrange for a **na›akai** which will attract a large throng of people, whereas the first kind is a more private affair.

On the whole, however, the classification of major and minor Navaho ceremonials does not offer definite lines of demarcation and is difficult to uphold. It seems to me safer to follow the native system which classifies ceremonials as one-night, three-, five- and nine-night performances. In this latter class there is a choice of a close of the ceremonial within the family circle as it were. Or a close with more elaborate performances for the public in general.

Several Navaho ceremonials require the appearance of **γé›i·** or masked impersonators in various functions. The term **γé·›** is frequently used to express scarcity, fear, so that the relativized form **γé›i·** suggests a 'terrible' one. But this translation of a 'terror' which **na·γé·›** 'enemy terror' seems to suggest does not appeal to informants for **γé›i·**, though the stem **-γé·›** is identical. Their thought appears to be that the **γé·›i·** are benevolent and helpful, whereas the **na·γé·›** are harmful beings which had to be slain and destroyed.

Informants suggest, therefore, that the **γé›i·** are in a class by themselves and are not concerned with the **na·γé·›** who, in turn, are the specific concern of **na·γé·› ne·zγání** the *slayer of enemy terrors* or Monster Slayer. The **γé›i·** are exact opposites of these

na·γé·ʾ and should be preserved for the benefit of the human (Navaho) race, not destroyed. No translation of the term is offered by natives so that we propose to use either the Navaho form **γéʾi·** or anglicized ye-i.

I have as a matter of course, consulted various native informants, beginning in 1908 with the late **giši·ṅ biγeʾ** *Son of late Cane* of Sanders, Arizona, and continuing with men like **xastˣi·n xatˣa·łí** Mr. Singer, his pupils Slim Curly and **yo·ʾe· xatˣałí** Beadway Singer of Greasewood Springs, Arizona, and others.

Interpreters too have varied. But I am chiefly indebted to the late Frank Walker and to my intimate friend of long standing, Albert G Sandoval, of Lukachukai, Arizona, for time and patience contributed in this study. Throughout the years I have left the drawings of the masks as the late Cane's Son made them without alterations, though other informants disagreed on points.

On **ƛé·ǯí** Nightway we have a full account of the Origin Legend and the nine-night ceremonial in: Washington Matthews, The Night Chant, a Navaho Ceremony, American Museum of Natural History, Memoirs, vol. 6 (1902).

Several writers have recorded the legend as, James Stevenson, Ceremonial of Hasjelti Dailjis, Eighth Annual Report of the Bureau of American Ethnology 228-85 (1891); S. Curtis, The North American Indian 1. 111-6; Mary C. Wheelwright, Tleji or Yahbechai Myth, The House of Navajo Religion, Bull. 1 (Santa Fe, New Mexico, 1938); Sapir-Hoijer, Navaho Texts, The Visionary, An Origin Legend of the Night Chant, 136-259, Linguistic Society of America, Iowa City, Iowa, 1942.

The γéʾi·

ƛé·ǯí *Nightway* is distinctly a **γéʾi·** ceremonial, because these supernaturals appear to conduct and control most of its phases. In other words, almost at any ceremony one wonders which **γéʾi·**

will perform. For convenience numerals are employed for the various **γé'i·**, though this does not mean that they must follow this numerical sequence at all times, nor must they be rated accordingly in importance. Apparently one **γé'i·** may function independently of the other and, if there are groups like male and female **γé'i·**, representatives of these groups may be selected for specific functions, at least in Nightway.

In this ceremonial we find these **γé'i·** which equate with masked impersonators:

1. **xaščéłtˣi'í** talking god;
2. **xaščé'o·γą·n** calling god;
3. **xaščé bᵃką'** (all told) 6 male hashch-e;
4. **xaščé ba'á·d** 6 female hashch-e;
5. **xaščéšžini·** black god;
6. **na·γé·' ne·zγání** monster slayer;
7. **tˣó bážíščíní** born-for-water;
8. **tˣó neinili·** water carrier, who is also mentioned as **xaščéłbái** gray god, and **xaščé dódí** the **dódí** hashch-e;
9. **γą̂· 'askidi·** hump back;
10. **zaxado·lžahí** fringed mouth, either right half of body red or yellow, with names corresponding;
11. **xaščéłčí·'** red hashch-e;
12. **xá·dačiši·** destroyer;
13. **xaščé 'ídí·łcǫ·sí** whistling hashch-e.
14. **xaščé'ołťohí** shooting hashch-e.

The sequence is arbitrary and even native informants are not bound by it, except that nos. 1 and 2 are mentioned in the lead, and 3 and 4 appear to be inseparable just as 6 and 7 are usually mentioned together. Other **γé'i·** than these appear singly for specific purposes.

A glance at the list of **γé'i·** reveals that not all of them are named **xa·ščé (xaščéh)** which is an hieratic term coined, as we have seen in the origin legend of the **γé'i·**, to express 'speechless.' All of them 'tried but failed to speak' (**č̓é·h xa·ʒí·'**). The late Son of the late Cane, the late Slim Curly and recently Beadway Singer are agreed on this point, though it is hard to explain why some **γé'i·** are called **xaščé** others not.

In English however the term 'god' has been employed for **xaščé** as, **xaščéšžini·** black god, **xaščé bᵃką'** male god, and so on. This was done for convenience rather than for accuracy and, for lack of anything better, is still retained. Personally I do not hesitate to employ anglicized hashch-e since this form conveys about as much as the English 'god' does for these supernaturals.

Since natives appear to be unable to establish the identity of the various **γé'i·** and hashch-e the relevant legends may be consulted. Briefly the **γé'i·** antedate the creation of the human race and appear as helpful mentors as soon as humans appear. In the Nightway incident (if we follow the Sapir-Hoijer Texts) the **γé'i·** appear to be identified with Bighorn People who disguise their identity under the form of bighorns and clothe the visionary in this form of a bighorn in order to instruct him in Nightway. They are therefore **diγin dine'é** Holy People, who may change their human forms at will.

In sandpaintings the **γé'i·** are represented in human form only, as far as known. The masked impersonators too are humans who represent the **γé'i·** in visible human form. The **γé'i·** both in sandpaintings and as masked beings are believed to visit the home of the patient in person. Therefore an impersonator of any **γé'i·** is not allowed to speak in the masks. If he did he would eventually go blind, suffer throat infection, and the loss of speech, or become even paralyzed and temporarily lose the use of his limbs.

This is hinted in the general scheme of Nightway and associated **xaščécohe·** big-godway ceremonials. Disregard of the **γé'i·** results in cripples, in blind, speechless or persons defective in speech.

Darkness, typified by night, settles upon the victim, hence the Nightway ceremonial is invoked. The **γé'i·**, as a matter of course, prefer the hours after sunset till dawn for their appearance, and that too may account for the name Nightway, at least to some extent. But they also perform in broad daylight and sandpaintings of them are made in daytime only.

The ceremonial always begins in the evening and that marks the first of nine nights of the ceremonial. Matthews calls this the first day as he follows the American method of reckoning by days, not the Navaho method of reckoning their ceremonials by nights. Thus **ƛé·ʒí** Nightway is usually a **ná·xásťái ƛé·' xatˣá·l** a nine-night ceremonial. We have then only eight days in which ceremonies are performed, as the first night opens the ceremonial, the ninth night closes it. On the whole however Dr Matthews has given us a very detailed account which can be safely followed.

The First Night.

The first night opens with **cᵃbą̨s yáží (γʷoltˣá·d)** *unraveling of small hoops* by the **γé'i·**. M. mentions twelve small hoops

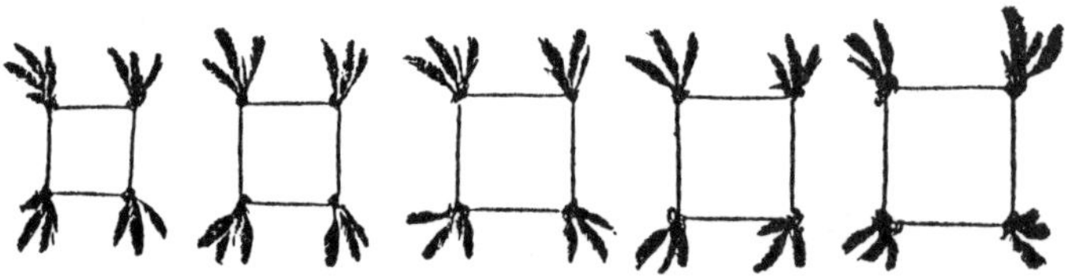

Hoops for Unraveling.

made of sumac twigs to which a cotton cord is tied, then wrapped over the hoop with slip knots which will easily release when the end of the cord is pulled. Four and sometimes five **γé'i·** perform at this unraveling ceremony and in this order: either

(1) (4) (8) (4) or

(1) (4) (8) (4) (8)

This presents three possibilities. Talking god (1) should not engage ordinarily in unraveling the small hoops. That should be the function of the female mask (4) who alternates with **xaščé dódí** or **xaščéłbái** (8) gray god who, in this action is called **xaščé dódí** the **dódí** hashch-e because he accompanies his movements with a **dódí, dódí** call. Either one or two **xaščé dódí** (8) may function as unravelers with female hashch-e (4).

The patient during the ceremonial is called the **bik̓ixatˣâ·li·** one over whom the sing is held. During the preparation of the small hoops he may leave the hogan but is called inside as soon as they are completed. He sits in the west of the room with legs extended. Talking god (1) enters with his **ba'álí·l** specialty or symbol which is a quadrangular contrivance. The four sticks are three spans in length and tied together with cord at the four corners where a downy feather is attached. The cords allow the quadrangle to be closed and opened by the operator. Talking god first lets it down to the patient's waist giving his call. He removes it from the patient and closes it with a sunwise motion bringing his right arm under his left arm which he swings to his right.

Next he opens the quadrangle and lowers it to the patient's chest again giving his call. He then removes it and again closes it. When opened again he lowers it to the shoulders of the patient repeating his hu-hu-hu-hu--call then removes and closes the quadrangle as before. Next he opens it and lowers it over the patient's head repeating his call, closes the quadrangle and leaves the hogan with it. This completes the first sanctification of the patient.

As soon as Talking god has left the first female hashch-e enters. One of the small hoops is given to (her or) him (if a man personates this γé'i·). Holding it with boths hands he applies it to the patient's soles, his knees below the kneecap, the hands outstretched on the knees, his chest, back, right and left shoulder, top of the head, right and left cheek then, holding the hoop to the patient's mouth with one hand he unravels the cord with the other. He then lets the hoop drop and since the cord has been tied to the hoop he drags it through the dirt as he leaves the hogan. Whether personated by a man or woman the female mask utters no call.

xaščéłbái the gray god or hashch-e now enters and is called hashch-e **dódí** because he accompanies the application or pressing of the hoops to the patient's body parts with his dod-, dod-call. He and the following female mask repeat the same actions as the preceding female mask had done even to dragging the hoop through the dirt. Should there be a second hashch-e **dódí** (8) he presses and unravels the small hoops as his predecessors have done. He too accompanies each pressing with his dod-, dod-call.

Should there be 4 masks, 2 of (4) and 2 of (8) each one repeats the same actions three times. In the event of two female and one hashch-e **dódí** masks they repeat four times unless Talking god should join them. But he usually performs with the closed quadrangular sticks. This practically closes the ceremonies of the first night.

The First Day.

The following morning which is reckoned the first day is devoted to cutting prayersticks. The **γé'i·** do not function in this ceremony, but Talking god and one of the hashch-e **ba'á·d** female gods don their masks and trimmings and giving his usual call Talking god proceeds to the sweat house, the female god following him.

At the sweat house Talking god throws back the blanket curtain of the entrance and, with his call or by signs, beckons to the patient to come out. He does so and sits in front of the sweat house legs outstretched. The two **γé'i·** walk around him four times, then receive plumed wands from the singer. Four black ones which had been planted on the north side of the sweat house are given to the Talking god, four blue ones from the south side to the female god. These they hold two in each hand and each masked person then presses the various body parts from the soles of the feet to the head, Talking god taking the lead. Both then give their calls into both ears of the patient four times, then return the plumed wands to the singer and recede to a secluded spot where they remove their masks, then rejoin the sweat house group to file back to the hogan with the patient.

The procedure does not differ essentially if heating in a pit is substituted for the sweat house. Sanctification with the plumed wands by the masked persons always follows. If pains are local such body parts receive special pressure treatment. M.[17] mentions special eye treatments with parts of bighorns or Rocky Mountain sheep held in the hands of the γé'i· during the pressing ceremony (p. 79)

In the afternoon a small sandpainting is drawn to represent the four sacred mountains. The central figure of pollen represents **tˣádídį· 'aški·** pollen boy for a man, **'añłťáni 'aťé·d** cornbeetle girl for a woman. Leading to the central figure is a cornmeal line, white for a man, yellow for a woman. Right and left footprints are added two on each side of the line. The patient is then called and instructed to step on each of the four footprints and to sit on the figure facing east or the doorway, his legs outstretched. The **ʒił biγi·n** mountain songs are then sung during which the **xaščé·łtˣi'í** Talking god enters.

He walks around the patient four times and shouts his call into each ear of the patient as he makes the circle. Then he seats himself at the left of the patient facing east. After a lengthy prayer which the patient repeats after the singer Talking god takes some soil from the miniature mountain at the east of the drawing and applies this to the patient's body parts accompany-

[17] M. is abbreviated for Matthews and (bracketed) numbers refer to pages in his Night Chant.

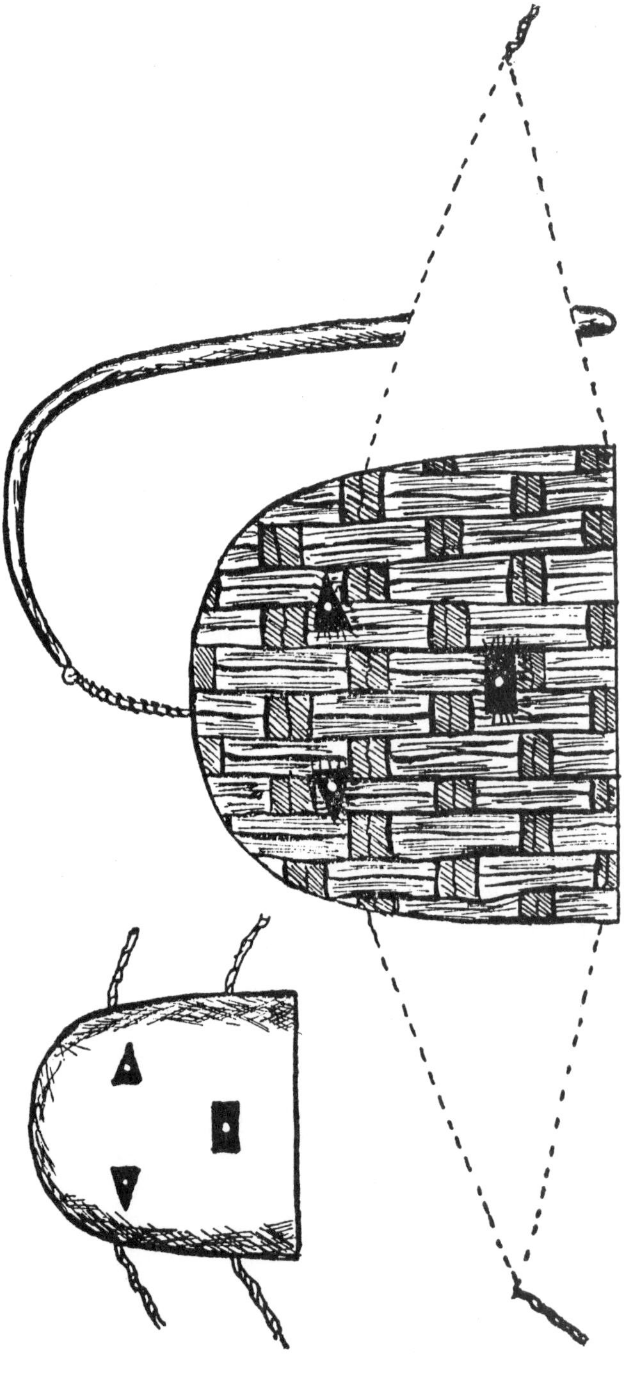

Face Masks and Sapling.

ing each application with his call. He repeats the application with soil from the mountain in the south, west and north then leaves the hogan to remove his mask and trappings.

The Second Night

The afternoon and evening are spent in getting trappings ready for the second night. If a **čó ʼéʼʼ** spruce garment is to be cut up the **tˣaogiš** 'cutting in places' ceremony will be performed. If there is to be **ʼaceʼʼ γʷoltˣá·d** tail feather unraveling these wreaths or bands too must be prepared for the patient.

And, because the coming ceremony appears to be designed to right any carelessness with masks, such as speaking in them, putting them on wrong and the like, a **ni·ké̆hé** face print or mask is to be made. If a male patient the face print should be made of a **tˣádi·gai** antelope fawn skin, if a female patient it is made of braided yucca leaves in the round shape of masks into which holes are punctured for eyes and mouth. Then triangular marks are made over the eye punctures and a square one over the mouth puncture.

Thongs are provided on the face masks, either of yucca or other material for tieing them to the patient's head. Nowadays antelope fawn skins are scarce and substitutes, either of spruce or yucca, will be made for male face masks. This is a concession of course to modern environment. But the essential part of the ceremony is preserved which is to have **na·yéʼʼ ne·zγání** Monster Slayer (6) and **tˣó bážíščíní** Born-for-water (7) perform the **tˣaogiš** cutting of the masks ceremony.

It matters little then that there may be a choice between **čó ʼéʼʼ** spruce garment and **ʼaceʼʼ γʷoltˣá·d** tail feather unraveling. In either event the **tˣaogiš** cutting (of the masks) must take place. The cutting of the spruce garment is merely combined with cutting of the masks, whereas unraveling of the tail feather garlands is accessory to cutting of the masks. Cutting of the face masks precedes cutting of a spruce garment and unraveling of tail feather trappings. Cutting of these face masks would seem essential, especially since the performers exercise especial care in ascertaining that all braided joints have been cut in the process.

The fact too that these bits of cut joints are dropped over the patient's head after the cutting process adds emphasis to the importance of the mask print rather than to those of other accessories like spruce garment or tail feather unravelings. However there may be variant practices, especially since the **tˣádi·gai** antelope fawn skins for the male mask are not always available. In such an event the space for the face is filled in with spruce twigs which are then ready for the **tˣaogiš** cutting ceremony.

The masked monster slayer motions with **bibé·ž** 'his arrowpoint knife' from below upward before he makes the actual incision. Born-for-water motions downward with his knife before he makes an incision. But both performers accompany the incisions with the call peculiar to them, just as most other **γé'i·**, masked impersonators, do in Nightway.

It is known that Monster Slayer and Born-for-water appear in most, if not all, chantway ceremonials. But their impersonators are not masked as they are in **ƛé·ʒí** Nightway though, like here, they may perform the **tˣaogiš** cutting and similar ceremonies. In Nightway however they are numbered among the **γé'i·** and must appear masked. In Nightway mask sets therefore special masks are provided for Monster Slayer and his brother Born-for-Water, though they never appear as dancers. They act however as **γé'i·** meaning that they may not speak in their masks but give their call only. Possibly they are masked in this ceremonial to inspire fear against offenses to the masks which we have pointed out above, and that too may be emphasized in this cutting ceremony which severs the hold a **γé'i'** or mask may have on the patient.

This hold extends beyond actualities of the individual. His or her prenatal periods enter into what is known to the Navaho as the **biǯíłté** complex or he (she) 'resembles' it. For example, some ceremonies require that the assistant rub his hands in white clay after every function. A child which is born to such an assistant later may show white spots on its arms and hands. And because the ye-i bichai daubs his body freely with white clay for his performances the child is said to **γé'i· bičai biǯíłté** (it) 'resembles' the ye-i bichai.

The same may result if during the period of pregnancy husband or wife look at sandpaintings, prayersticks, eclipse of sun or moon, and the like. The phenomena may later cause a resemblance to them in the child. Techniques like cutting or unraveling spruce and herb garments, feather bundles, and here in Nightway of cutting masks are designed to remove the 'hold' which supernaturals have secured on mortal men through their faulty behavior. The two Slayers are usually chosen to perform this cutting and in Nightway they must be masked.

The Second Morning.

The morning is devoted to the preparation of prayersticks which are to be sacrificed to the **γé'i·** who will appear in the **na·'akai** on the last night. Prominent are the two **kiní·' na'ígai-(gi) ƙe·ťą̨·** the prayersticks at-the-white-across-house-center. This designates the White House ruin in Canyon de Chelley which is believed to be the home of **γé'i·**, particularly of **xaščéłtˣi'í** Talking god and **xaščé'o·γa·n** Calling god. Talking god leads every dancing group in the last night's exhibitions, but does not dance. Calling god is leader of the **'acáłeh** first dancers, who open the performances of the closing night. He also leads other groups who perform throughout the night and their performances go by the general name of **na·'akai** or **na'akai** 'here and there groups go.'

To these dancers prayerstick offerings are made, meaning that these sacrificial offerings are made to the γé'i· **b·ką'** male ye-i and the γé'i· **ba'á·d** female ye-i as a sort of invitatory sacrificial offering to induce them to appear in the final dances. The offerings are deposited at the base of a steep rock after a prayer has been said to them. In this prayer **xaščéłtˣi'í** Talking god is invoked, then **xaščé'o·γa·n** Calling god, then **xaščé b·ką'** Male god, then **xaščé ba'á·d** Female god, so that one stick is offered to the entire male group, one to the entire female group of γé'i·. Although **xaščéłbái** Gray god appears with every group of male and female dancers at the **na'akai** no prayerstick is made for him.

After completion of the prayerstick ceremony the sweat bath is again performed and the same masked γé'i· (1) and (4) sanctify the patient as on the preceding day.

The Third Night

yo·'e· xat'a·łí Beadway Singer of Greasewood Spring, Arizona, who is also a recognized interpreter of **xé·ǯí** Nightway, performs the **'ił ya'iltˣá·d** ceremony on the third night of the ceremonial. The term designates 'it has been caused to bound up from one' and is descriptive of the entire ceremony. Early in the morning preceding this night a plume is attached to a spruce sapling and allowed to remain there the entire day.

At dusk this sapling is brought inside the hogan and planted in front of the patient. The plume is removed from the sapling, but a long cord is provided on it. This cord will be attached to a face mask loosely tied to the patient. The face mask is again made of a **tˣádi·gaí** antelope fawn skin for a male patient, of yucca for a female patient. The cord on the sapling is attached to the mask. The sapling is bent over to it in doing so. Then it is released and the rebound of the sapling lifts the mask from the patient's face, after an assistant has released the cords which secure the mask to the face in back of the head.

As the sapling snaps back into position it will take the mask with it and remove any eye trouble. Obviously somebody must manipulate the sapling. Beadway singer holds that **xaščé·o·γa·n** (2) manipulates the removal of the **tˣádi·gai** fawn mask for a man, whereas the first female γé·i· (4) manipulates it for a woman patient.

Others let **xaščéłtˣi·í** (1) and a **xaščé ba·á·d** (4) perform this tree ceremony which Matthews assigns to the fourth night before the vigil (p. 103). On the whole however the tree mask-lifting ceremony does not differ and must be performed by two γé·i·.

The Third Day.

The morning is occupied in preparing prayersticks some of which are offered to the **·acáłeh** first dancers of the ninth night. At the sweat house **(tˣáčé·h)** the same two γé·i· sanctify the patient as on previous mornings. The better part of the afternoon is spent in the preparation of **ke·tą· łání** many prayersticks

Twelve white ones are lined up on the east bottom of a native basket, twelve blue ones on the south bottom, twelve yellow ones on the west bottom, twelve black ones on the north basket bottom. Facets are cut on the female sticks with eye and mouth marks, whereas the six male sticks of each cardinal point have the regular hood of male sticks with no face marks. The entire lot are of solid wood like mountain mahogany or wild cherry and are not intended to receive tobacco, feathers, or the like. No designs are painted on their body colors.

In the center of the basket four **ke·tą·** made of reed joints are imbedded in cornmeal. As the reed joints are hollow they should serve as tobacco containers with feather plugging and sealing after the patient has symbolically lighted them with rock crystal held to the sun. The white cigarette is for **xaščéłtˣi·í** (1), the blue one for a **xaščé ba·á·d** (4), the yellow one for a **xaščé bˣką·**

(3), the black one for **xaščé ʼołťohí** (13) shooting hashch-e (M. p. 94, par. 403). He says 'these are a divine company of **xaščé ʼayôi** (his Hastseayuhi *ib.*) of which the wooden pieces are for the minor divinities of the group, the cigarettes for (the major or) superior ones.'

He then assigns these **γéʼi·** to apply the 52 sticks to the patient each entering four times in turn: 1, 4, 8, 4. The two 4s do not utter a call when they apply the sticks to the body parts, but **xaščé dődí** (8) and no 1 do. No. 1 also applies his quadrangular hoop over the patient to open the application of prayersticks and again to close the ceremony. M. following his singer informants assigns this ceremony to the third night, whereas Beadway Singer, following Mister Singer, assigns it to the fourth night to precede the **γéʼi· bicą́ ʼálné·h** 'making the food' of the **γéʼi·** or feeding the masks as this ceremony is popularly known.

This same school of singers seems to hold that **xaščéłtˣiʼí** Talking god should apply his **baʼálí·l** especial symbol of power, the quadrangular hoop, and allow other applications to the patient to be made by other **γéʼi·**. An example of this is found in applying the **cᵃbą·s yáží** or small hoops on the first night. There the leader (1) allows nos. 4, 8, 4, 8 to apply the twelve small hoops to the patient and merely opens the ceremony and closes it with his own larger hoop. He repeats the same on this occasion, then allows nos. 4, 8, 4, 8 to apply the prayersticks to the body parts of the patient, after which he closes the ceremony by again applying his quadrangular hoop over the patient.

The Fourth Night.

γéʼi· bicą́ ʼálné·h

The ye-i's Food is Prepared.

After dark the **do·ʼi·γá·ž** no-sleep or vigil is observed meaning that persons are not supposed to sleep during the entire night.

At the very start of this vigil all masks are lined up in the rear of the hogan space in this order:

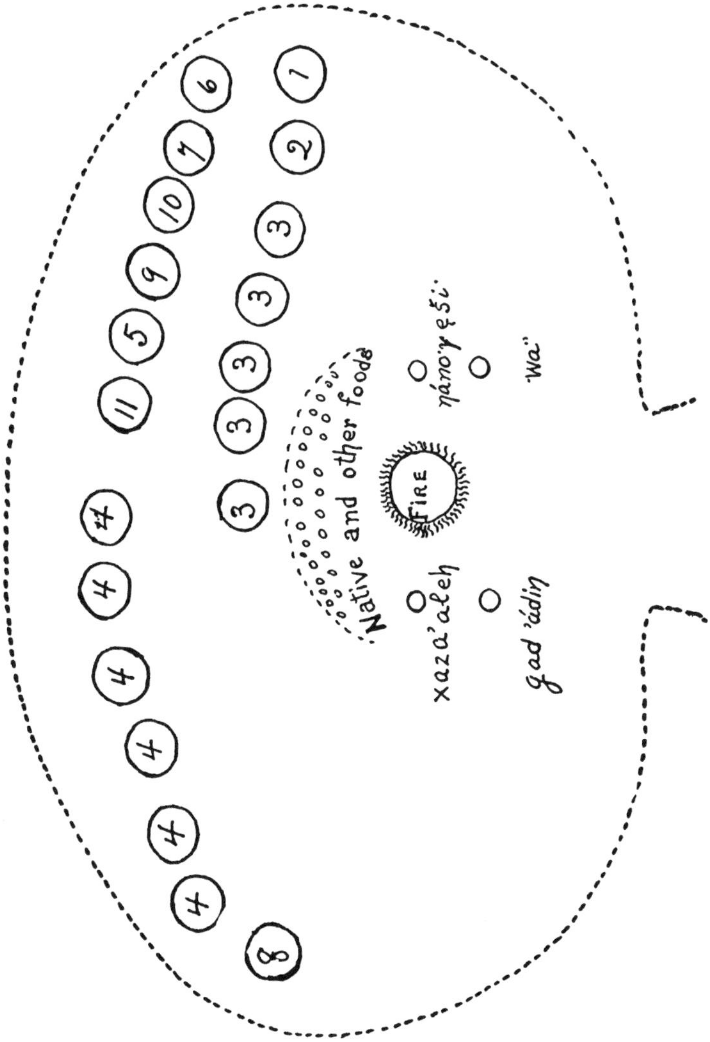

Feeding The Masks.

Our informant like other singers holds that these four native foods must be set down near the fireplace, but mentions that the dish of **wa·›** beeweed greens is set down first. It is followed by **náno·γęši·** 'spread out' small round breads or cakes, then by **xaza›ale·h** *Sp. shimaha*, rock parsley, and last by **gad ›ádin** no cedar mush.

After that other native foods, biscuits baked in ashes, paper bread, slap cakes, meats and nowadays even canned goods are lined up between the masks and the fireplace. A boy and a girl are then instructed to perform the **tˣó biƙéltˣah** asperging them with water. After that they are told to feed each mask with a mush made of **našǯį́ší** small sweet corn which has been pit-roasted then ground into cornmeal and mixed with water. Thus a pure food is fed to the masks by a virgin boy and girl.

A pinch should then be taken from all the foods and put to the mouth of every mask, starting with 1 and ending with 8 as the **xaščéłbái** gray hashch-e mask is always set down last. After this ceremony has been completed, which is known as **γé›i· bicą́ ›álné·h** the ye-i or masks are fed, all present except the patient and singer may partake of the same and other foods available.

The remainder of the night is spent awake and with singing. Most of the songs are not sung with rattle accompaniment, which means that the **xóžǫ́·ǯí ǯiš** or **ʒiłe·ž** Blessingway pouch or mountain soil is held in the singer's and other hands (if they have such bags of mountain soil) during these songs. No rattle or drum may accompany these songs.

M. also describes smoking of the masks by the singer who blows wild mountain tobacco on each mask. Also shaking the masks when the singer raises each one and rocks them slightly sideways (p. 110). In addition two prayersticks are cut during the night. The use to be made of them accounts for their names: **čaxałxe·ł ba·ítˣįh** (stick) 'to be given to darkness' and **xayołká·ł ba·ítˣįh** to be given to dawn. Appropriate songs dedicate these sticks not necessarily Blessingway songs. The darkness stick however is carried out that night, the dawn stick at dawn after this fourth night.

The Fourth Day.

NIGHTS— X X X X X X X X X – 9

DAYS— † † † † † † † † – 8

If we follow the Navaho system of counting nights of a ceremonial rather than days consumed we'll find that the day is of little importance in counting. Thus on this morning of the 4th day of the ceremonial the Navaho will say: **ʼašλaʼ xaʒih** there are five left, meaning that the ceremonial will last five more nights. This point should be recalled in reading Matthews' splendid account of Nightway. We follow the Navaho system of calling this the fourth day of the ceremonial which precedes its fifth night.

Practically the day has been introduced by the offerings of the preceding night of the darkness prayerstick and of the offering at dawn of the dawn prayerstick. The sweat house ceremony which is repeated for the last time is performed exactly as on the preceding mornings with the same ye-i functioning.

The Fifth Night.

Perhaps some of the singers and assistants who had to spend the preceding night sleepless will prefer to catch a bit of sleep after the sweat house ceremonies of the morning. After all the preparations for the evening and night do not require very elaborate effort. In prospect is a **xoʼdi·ƛá·d** 'swooning' ceremony and one of initiation, neither of which require much preparation.

If the **xoʼdi·ƛá·d** 'one is swooned' ceremony is asked for a small sandpainting, on which the figures of Talking, male and female gods are represented, is drawn. Talking god holds his **baʼálí·l** extended not closed, the female **γéʼi·** holds plumed wands in each hand, the male **γé'i·** is a companion to the other two.

At the proper time in the evening, after the patient is seated upon the sandpainting, a drum tap on a concealed up-turned native basket, summons the **γé'i·** to appear. Talking and the female god rush in with their calls in order to discern if the patient is frightened by their appearance. Usually that is the case because the patient is prepared for the test. He or she may approach the sandpainting over cornmeal footprints in a simulated semiconscious condition, half swooning one might describe it. He succumbs immediately to the fiction that the **γé'i·** are the cause. Hence Nightway is responsible and the **γé'i·** must correct the situation. Others may join the test even as mere spectators. Should they too swoon it indicates that for some reason or other this Nightway affects them.

That same night initiations are available for any children to: **γé'i· daʒiłcé·h** see the **γé'i·** . Grownups too may join to fill in their number of times up to four that they have seen the ye-i. Every good Navaho should see them four times in a lifetime. All participants are novices for the occasion and are treated alike by the performing **γé'i·**. This same initiation ceremony may be repeated on the sixth night, then on the afternoon of the sixth day and seventh night. But if requisitions for initiation are made on the morning of the eighth or last day of the ceremonial the singer may make an additional charge for this exception.

The initiation is always preformed by **xaščéłtˣi'í** (1) and one of the **xaščé ba'á·d** (4) though a man usually wears this mask. He (4) carries a fawn bag with cornmeal which he sprinkles upward on the soles, knees, waist, chest, back, shoulders, and head indicating thereby which parts (1) will strike with his two yucca leashes. The candidates are supposed to sit with downcast eyes and even with covered heads until told to look up. When they do they find that the ye-i have removed their masks and they find themselves looking into the faces of two well known friends.

The leashing with two yucca blades is hardly painful and is not intended to be so. It is rather preparatory to γé'i· **dazilcé·h** 'they see' and then know who the ye-i really are when they appear. That knowledge is for the initiated who know that the masked impersonators represent the real ye-i, though natives may be wearing their masks. The uninitiated should learn this for themselves! Hence the initiated will not divulge what they have learned at this ceremony.

After seeing who the ye-i are the female ye-i moves its mask to the face of each candidate and makes sure that the initiated look through the eye openings of the mask. This manipulation of the female mask appears to be part of the ceremony of 'seeing the ye-i' if not an essential part of it. There is, as a matter of course, no objection to a candidate who chooses to 'see the ye-i' twice or even three times in succession at one ceremonial, in order to fulfill a life's obligation of seeing them four times.

The Fifth Day.

Towards dawn a prayerstick is prepared which is called **cēní·ǯį' ni'ítˣįh** 'placing a stick at rock center.' After sunup the prayeratick is deposited somewhere in cliffs or bluffs as it is an offering to the γé'i· who supposedly dwell in **cēní·'** rock centers or cliffs and is an invitation to them to appear both in the sandpaintings and as masked personators on the following days. Possibly too it is an offering to the Rocky Mountain sheep whom γą̂·'**askidi** (9) humpback represents.

Any time of the fifth day is referred to by **dį́·'** **xaǯih** 'four remain' meaning that there *remain four nights* of the ceremonial. This fifth day, and the following sixth and seventh days are devoted to sandpaintings and, because these are elaborate affairs, the greater part of the morning and noon hours is required for them. The sanctification ceremonies after the completion of the drawings also require time.

There appears to be some latitude in choosing the **γéꞌiˑ** performer after the sandpainting has been completed. A **xaščé bᵉką'** male hashch-e should ordinarily perform. But, since **xaščé'oˑγaˑn** calling god (2) is the leader in the dance groups of the last night he may be asked to perform. In this event he wears the leading **γé'iˑ bᵉką'** male mask with two plumes either on the right or left side of the mask.

Should the patient request the sandpainting of **xaščé'oˑγaˑn** for the morning of the sixth day calling god (2) must then decorate his mask with twelve plumes when he performs over the patient. As the sandpaintings primarily represent some phase in the life of the ye-i the singer himself does not make the applications. It seems more fitting that this be done by one of the more prominent ye-i and **xaščé'oˑγaˑn** is chosen.

The application does not vary. After moistening his hands Calling god presses them on the feet of the figure and applies the soil to the feet of the patient accompanying this with his call. He repeats this same sanctifying process with other body parts by transferring them from all figures to the patient's body parts. His function is then completed and he leaves the hogan to remove his mask. Others in the hogan will gather meal and soil from the various figures and preserve them to be used at other ceremonials as **zaˑńił** medicine food.

The Sixth Night.

This night is again spent in initiating candidates, and the **'acáłeh** or first dancers continue rehearsals for their appearance on the last night. They need not be masked for these rehearsals, but the masks are trimmed and prepared for use on other days.

The Sixth Day.

The morning is devoted to making any sandpainting called for. If as said a sandpainting other than that of **xaščé'o·γa·n** is requested calling god performs over the patient masked with the ordinary male mask decorated with only two plumes on the side of the mask. It will be past noon when the sandpainting and performances over the patient are completed. The afternoon is partly devoted to practice rehearsals even on the strip cleared in front of the hogan for the last night's exhibition. Candidates for initiation and visitors, as dancing groups, continue to come in to make camp within easy reach of the dancing grounds.

The Seventh Night.

Initiation of candidates is performed as on the previous evening by the same masked personators, and dancing rehearsals of the **'acáłeh** continue under the direction of the conducting singer. The idea is that this **'acáłeh** first dancing groups will avoid any errors of omission in the songs which they must sing in the masks. The singer goes to considerable pains in instructing them. He himself is not masked and does not sing in a mask. He enjoins on the masked personators however that the words of the song must follow properly, otherwise the entire dance of the last night cannot be held.

Initiations of candidates are primarily held on the afternoon and evening of the 7th day and 8th night and should ordinarily be concluded then, as there is an extra fee to be paid to the singer if initiations are extended to the 8th day. This may happen to late comers from greater distances. The idea is that they could have made an earlier start.

The Seventh Day.

The morning is again occupied with a sandpainting. This is also the morning of γé'i·'aš. The term has been used by Matthews to define 'begging' gods who may be sent out on soliciting errands to neighboring or distant camps. Here the leader gives his call and the camp family head brings out a gift, small or large, as he sees fit or chooses. This soliciting expedition may begin on the sixth to eighth mornings while the **γé·i·** sandpaintings are being made at the hogan and contributions are felt to be made to the **γé·i·** who will appear at the last night dances, or even to those who are requested to appear especially.

It appears to me, from statements made by singers who had an extensive practice that **γé·i··aš** does not necessarily apply to 'begging' gods. They didn't seem to me to be begging when they called or gave their call outside of my home in years gone by. On one occasion I had no time to present a gift of tobacco and eatables. They ignored me because I was not ready. One can hardly say that the three ye-i who scour the neighborhood are really beggars. They solicit gifts, yes! But, if such gifts are not forthcoming they pass on to other camps. After all, the ye-i do not solicit for themselves but for the patient and his family, whose expenditure is undoubtedly heavy!

Perhaps we have a twofold **γé·i··aš**. The term appears to imply only two impersonators 'who leave' say on an errand. As now practiced **xaščéłtˣi·í** Talking god (1) leads the group of three ye-i, himself included, with a **xaščé bᵃką·** (3) male hashch-e and a **xaščé ba·á·d** (4) female hashch-e, though a **xaščéłbái** (8) may also accompany them. If so the term **γé·i··aš** 'two ye-i leave' does not seem to fit, unless we assume that only the male and female hashch-e are counted, and neither the leading Talking god (1) nor the buffoon gray god (8) count among the 'two' visiting ye-i.

There is some evidence for taking this view of the soliciting **γé·i··aš** group. There are really two solicitors of gifts since **xaščéłtˣi·í** merely leads the two and gives his call which the other

Color Plates

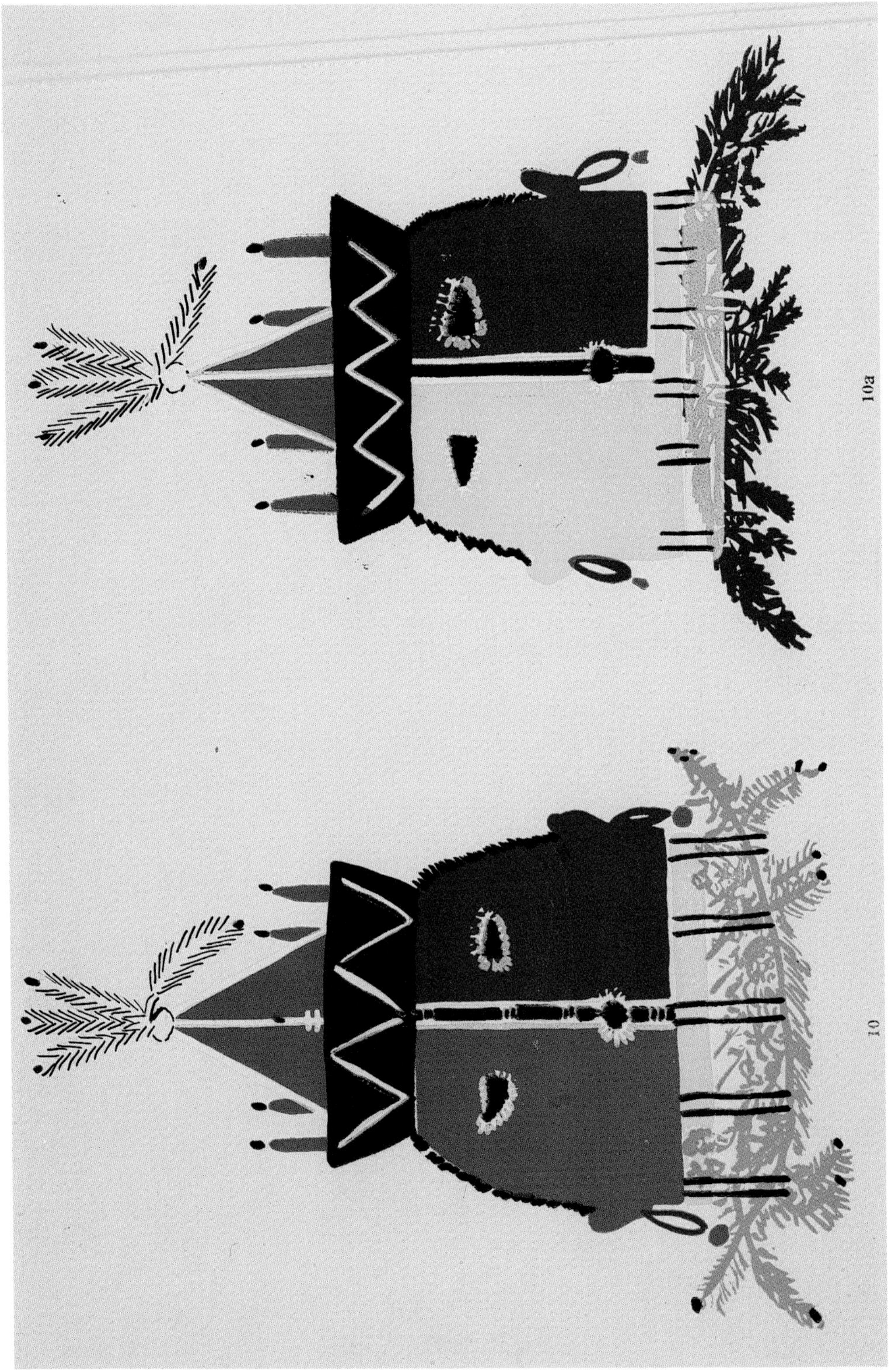

Red and Yellow Face of Fringed Mouth Masks

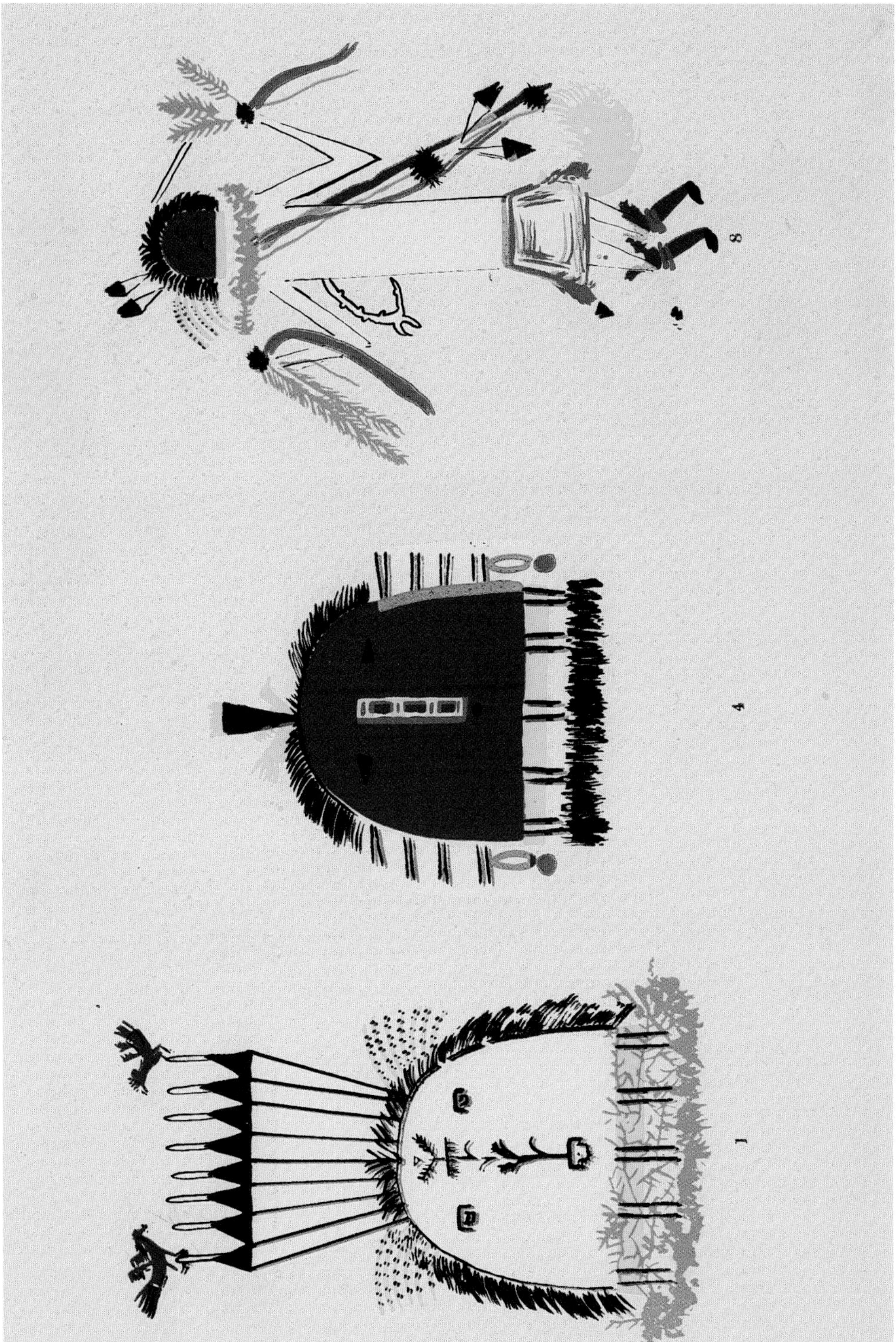

Talking god (1), Female god (4), and dódí hasch-e (8)

Mask of Black God (5)

OPPOSITE: Masks of Monster Slayer (6) and Born-for-Water (7)

6

7

Masks of Destroyer (12) and Red god (11)

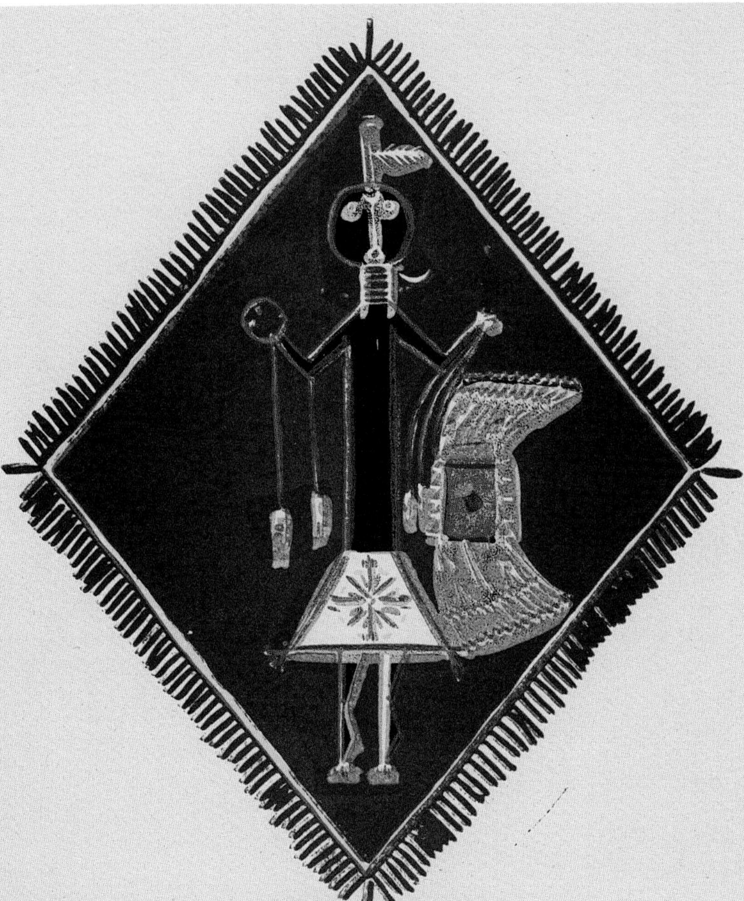

5

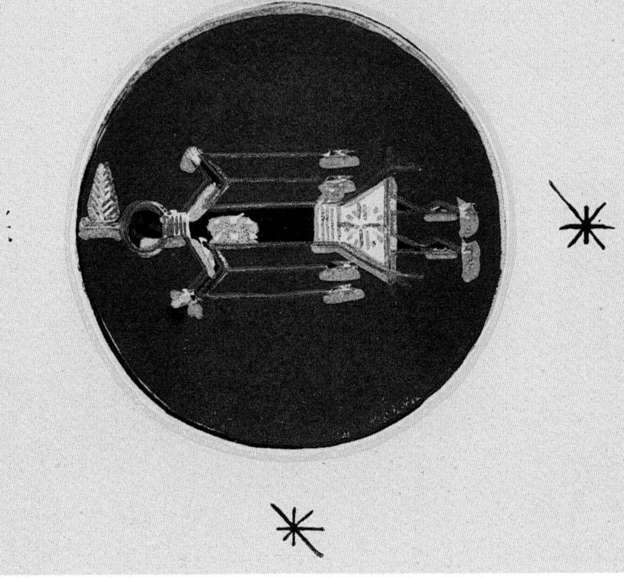

6

Black god (5) and Sun Figure (6)

14

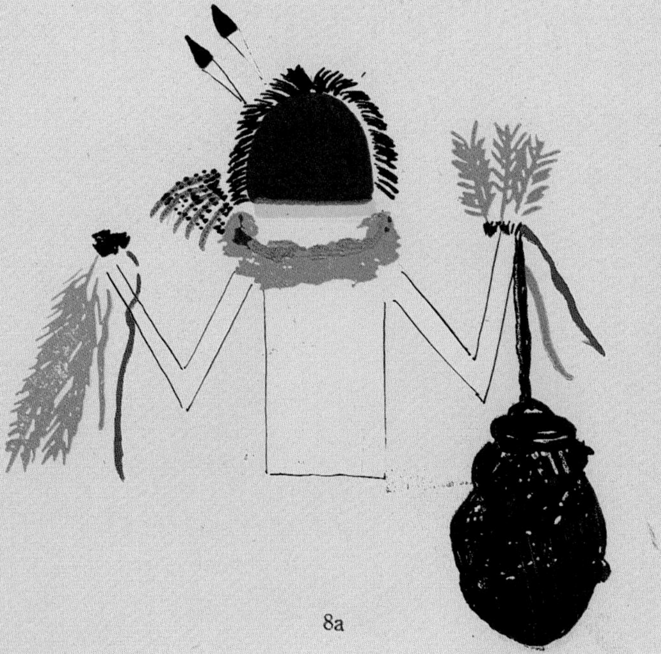

8a

Masks of Shooting hasch-e (14) and Water Sprinkler (8^{a})

OPPOSITE: Slim First Dancers (2,3)

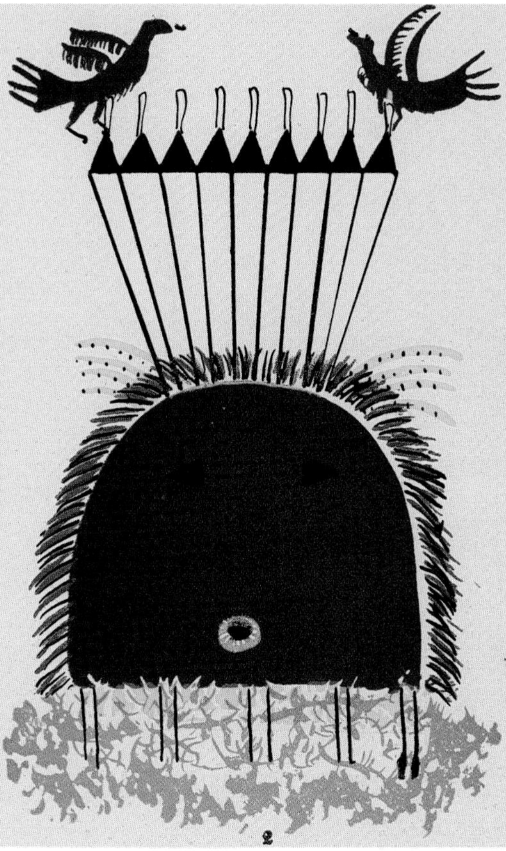

2

4

3

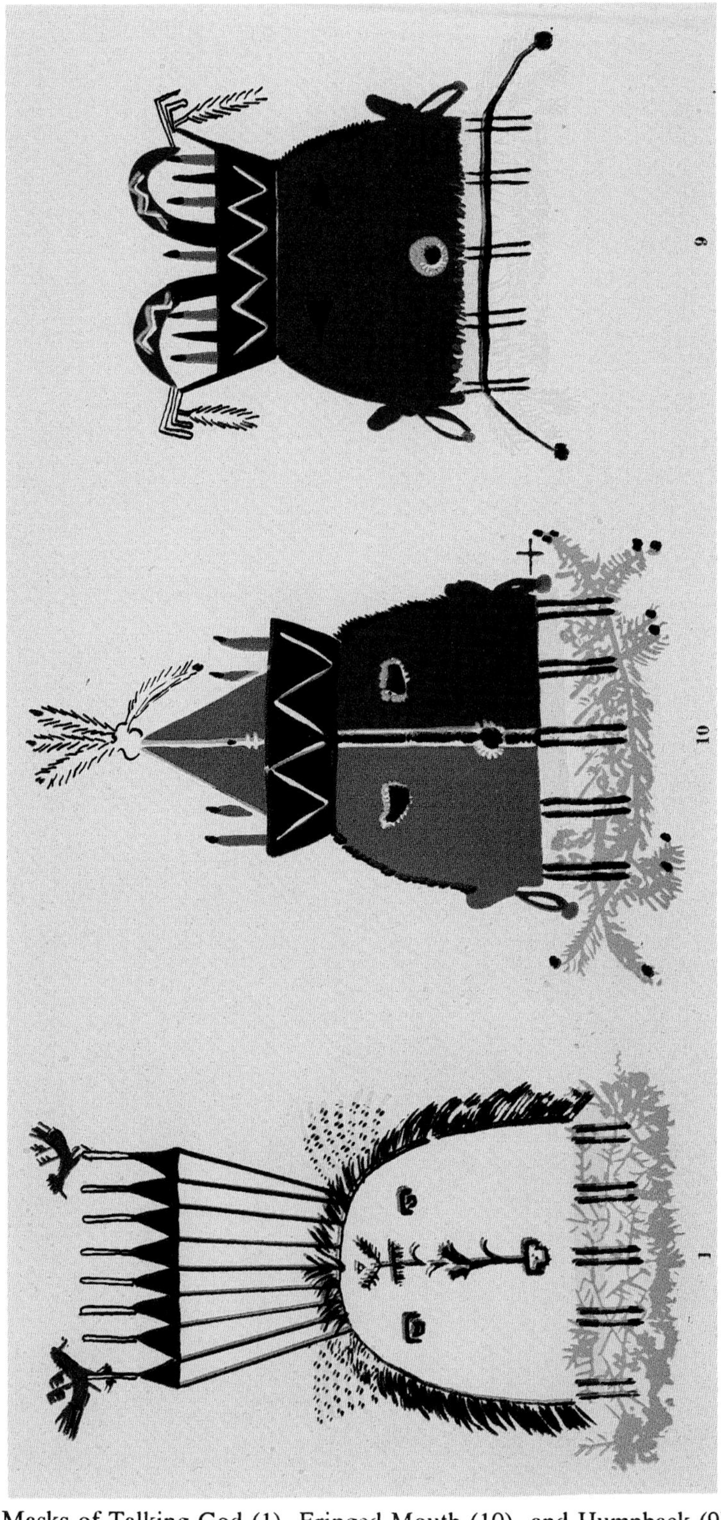

Masks of Talking God (1), Fringed Mouth (10), and Humpback (9)

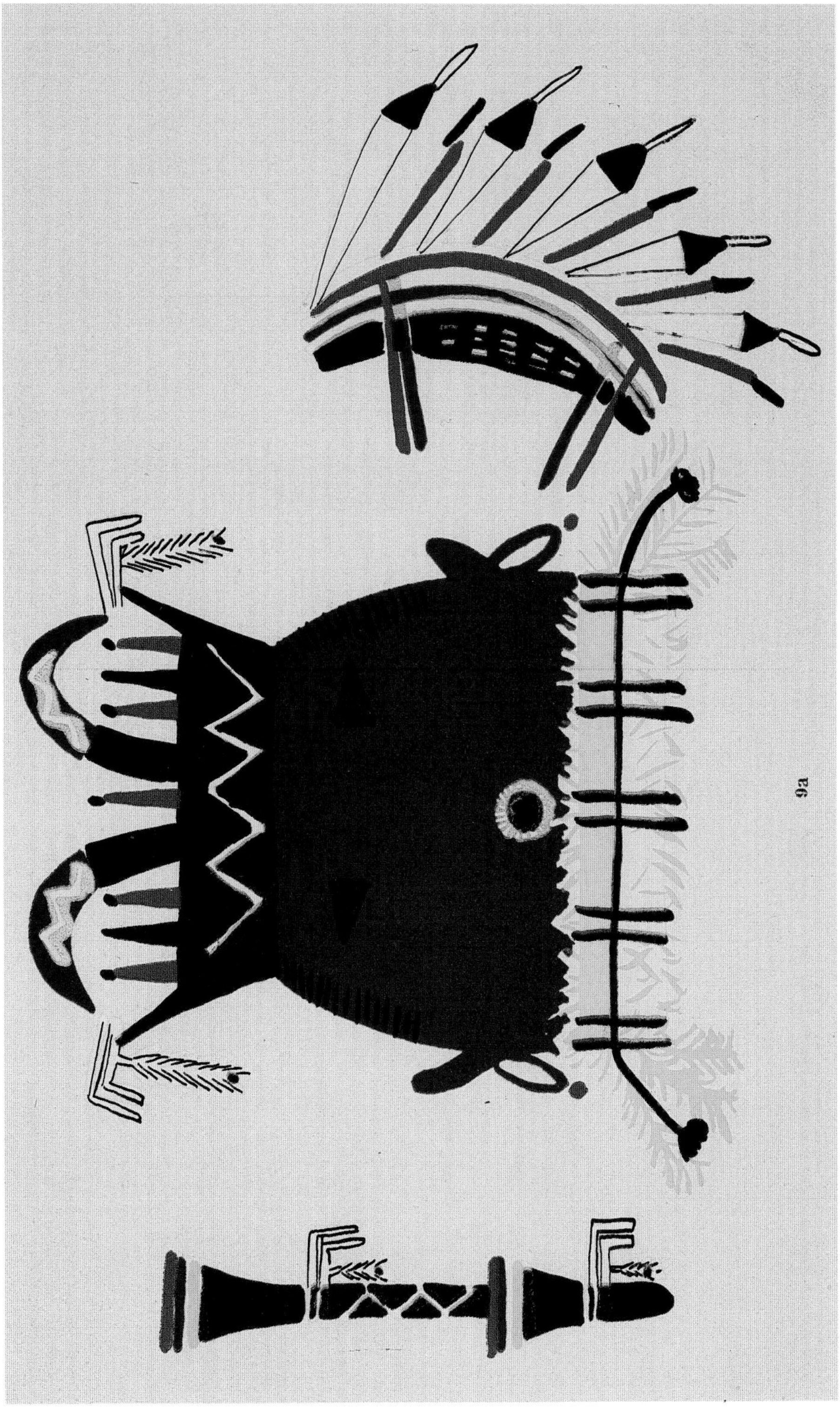

The Cane and Rainbow of Humpback (9[a])

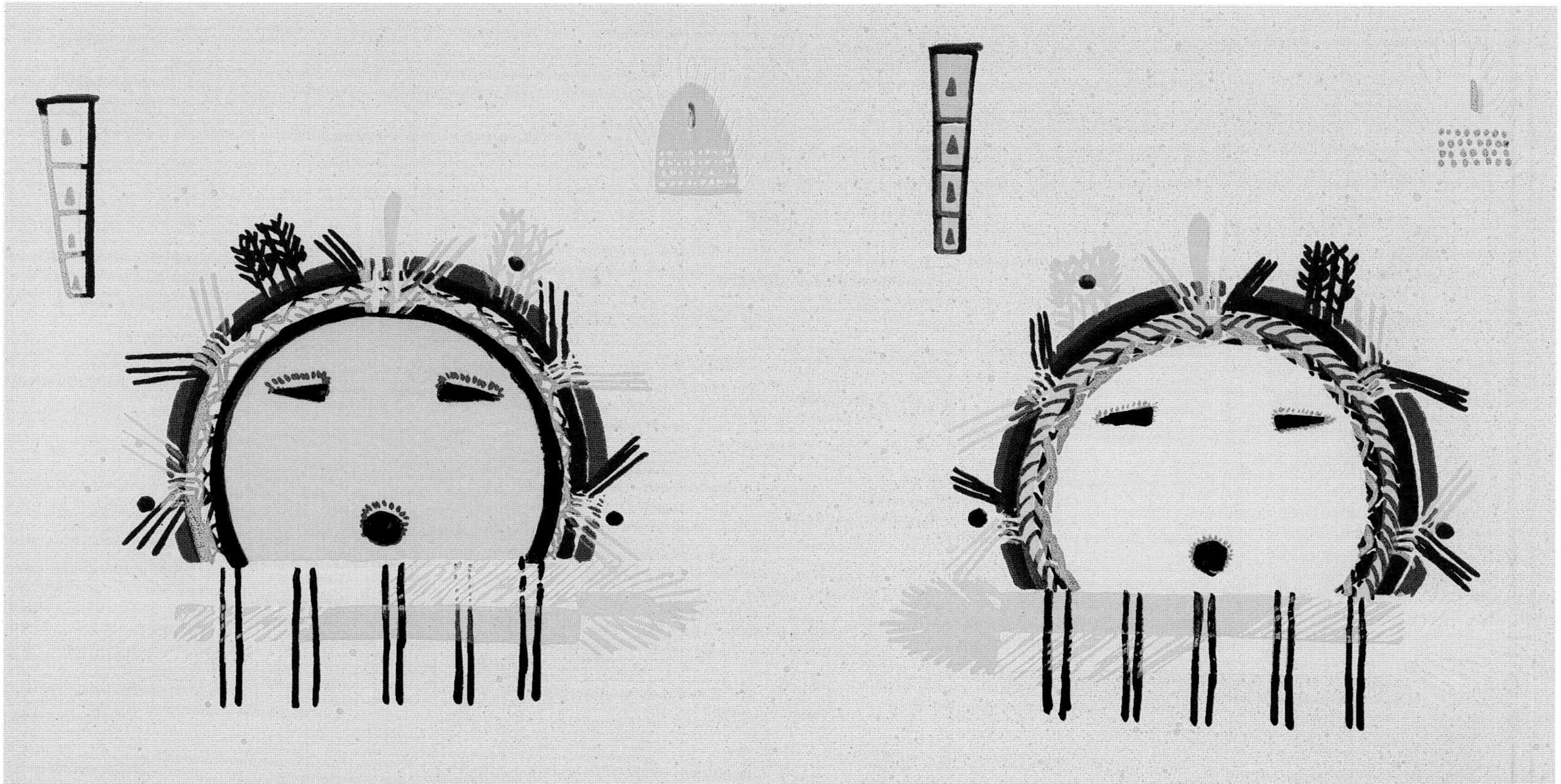

The ʼałké·ʼ na·ʼaši· Masks

two cannot do unless he is present. **xaščéłbáí** gray god accompanies the two main solicitors, and it is understood that he is more of a buffoon than main actor and may be dispensed with.

But at the ceremonial hogan there is more to **γé'i·'aš** than in this soliciting episode of the ye-i. Here we find that two distinct ye-i appear for the benefit of the patient, not to solicit gifts, but to perform especially over him. As these performers belong to the ye-i people, attending visitors are interested in their performances and may even request that they be 'sanctified' by them.

You have then **xaščéłtˣi'í** (1) who leads this **γé'i·'aš** group, and **zaxado·lžahí bošk̄i·ž łičí'ígí·** fringed mouth with one side red (10) and one **xaščé ba'á·d** female hashch-e (4) who merely follows the other two. **zaxado·lžahí** (10) really performs over the patient on this morning, that is, he applies the body parts of the sandpainting figures to the body parts of the patient. Then (1) leads him outside where he (10) sanctifies any petitioners by giving his call over them. The ye-i bichai (1) is then free again to lead the visiting **γé'i·'aš** to various camps.

The afternoon and evening are given to candidates who desire to be initiated.

The Eighth Night.

Visitors from distances have arrived and made camp near the dancing grounds. Initiation continues. From various camps one can hear dancing groups rehearsing, whereas at the ceremonial hogan singers and assistants are occupied in rehearsing the First Dancers, or in decorating and painting the masks for the final performances. Whoever is able to snatch a few hours sleep does so, to be prepared for the doings of the next day and closing night.

The Eighth Day.

Initiations should be finished by this time, but stragglers may pay the singer a fee to allow them to be initiated even on this last morning. The patient may request that **xaščéšžini·** black god perform over him that evening. If so the sandpainting of **xaš-čéšžini** is made now, but the man who personates him leaves the hogan in the morning and looks for a comfortable place where he sleeps all day. If the sandpainting is not made the black god does not appear.

If black god is to appear and perform over the patient that evening his sandpainting represents him standing in a diamond-shaped star at cardinal points, two of these figures, east and south, are called **xaščéšžini·** black god, those west and north are called **čošt'agí** 'inside thighs' from the fact that the insides of the thighs are colored red as against white of the east and south figures. The figures represent one and the same black god, only that his counterpart **čošt'agí** is upheld in sandpaintings. Even the face or mask part does not differ.

There is a white line running up from the mouth to slightly above the eyes where it is surmounted by a crescent. This was put on the mask by black god himself with soap root foam while the crescent shaped white shell represents his **biγe·l** offering made to him. Others hold that the crescent represents **šâit'ą̨** the new moon. This opinion seems to be in accord with the general o-pinion (also expressed in Origin legends) that black god is the maker of stars and constellations. It also is in accord with legendary accounts which assign making of the months to him and the new moon introduces a new month, so that the new moon should be a symbol of black god's assignment to make the months.

Commonly too it is held that, when black god had accepted the assignment to make and arrange the months he was found to have the Pleiades attached to his right ankle. He stamped his right foot on the ground which caused the Pleiad to hop to his knee. The next time he stamped his foot it hopped to his hip.

The third time it hopped to his shoulder, the fourth time it hopped to his head and located along his left temple as he desired.

Some singers locate Pleiad in this position on black god faces of his sandpainting (in Nightway) and also on his mask, meaning that they follow the sense of the legend in which black god had made this constellation to hop where he desired it. The four figures of his sandpainting should indicate this on their faces.

Other singers are satisfied to indicate the general configuration of the Pleiad at least on the faces of sandpainting figures (see cut p. 60): with a general outline of **yikáisdáhí** or milky way across their shoulders. This group of singers agree with the first group that black god made the constellations and months, but are not so much concerned about his hopping Pleiad as the first group is. At any rate, the black god is somehow connected with the months and new moon, Pleiad, Milky way and other constellations. Perhaps for that reason Nightway represents him in the center of four Big Stars in his sandpainting.

The center circle in blue of his sandpainting should represent the sun. Inside of it the figure of Monster Slayer is drawn to indicate that he is the son of the sun and as such belongs to the **γéʼi·** of Nightway. With the sun thus depicted, and the new moon represented with the Pleiad on the face of black god, not to mention the milky way across his shoulders, one can hardly escape making a connection, as the natives do, between black god and the starry heavens. Also that the Navahos consider sun and moon part of the constellations in the heavens originating from black god.

Legends, however, appear to let black god cover the heavens with stars after the carriers have been assigned to the sun and moon discs on their daily journeys. There is some hint however in Nightway songs and prayers that sun and moon carriers are included in the **γéʼi·** group of this chantway, though no specific masks are assigned to them except perhaps in the **na·γé·ˀ ne·z-γáni** monster slayer mask, as explained for the sandpainting mentioned above, where the figure of monster slayer is set in the center of the sun figure. His brother would be included, because born-for-water is never separated from monster slayer. The two are thought of as one. In Nightway, as in other ceremonials, the two appear jointly, for example, in the cutting ceremony mentioned previously.

At any rate, whether sun and moon belong to the **γéˀi·** and constellations or not, black god preserves his unconcern and independence of the rest of the group and spends the day in sleepful oblivion, while the rest are busy with other details. This attitude of the personator, at least, agrees with legendary accounts of the behavior of this supernatural in general. Visitors to the last night's performance will pay little attention to this solitary sleeper, though natives will soon learn that he will be the masked black god.

xá·da·či·ši· (12) is a name of obscure meaning. High **xá·-** is possibly a contraction of **xaná·-** out again, **da·-** may be used for 'thing' and **-či·š** also occurs in **k̓e·t̓ą· do·či·š** destroying prayerstick. We have tentatively called the mask 'destroyer' as that seemed to be the feeling Beadway Singer got of it.

He explained that a **k̓e·t̓ą· do·či·š** prayerstick is made, then broken into small fragments and dropped over the patient to drive the sickness away. Hence we get the 'pulverized' prayerstick and **xá·da·či·ši·** gets his name from this fact: he 'pulverizes' sickness, as it were, when he applies his yucca rod to sore body spots. Thus he may be called the 'destroyer', perhaps even pulverizer (of sickness).

The masked person wears the ordinary leading male mask (2) with the two feathers. His body is decorated with hoops as shown under his mask, but the last hoop is left open O O O O as shown.

He also has an improvised hoop strapped to his waist to indicate that he supervises the game of hoop-poling though the poles of this game are not shown. The hoop at his waist, however, indicates that he is in charge of the game if the ye-i play it, or if men happen to indulge in it on the grounds. He is a clownish sort of fellow and his pranks are enjoyed. He may whip people with his yucca leashes and even pretend to strike 'very hard' which means that he does not hurt them. With every stroke he gives his call.

There is little activity during the rest of the day. Most visitors are eager to secure a camp site along the space cleared in front of of the hogan for the masked dancers.

Masks of **xaščéłčí·ʼ** red hashch-e (11) and of **xá·da·či·ši·** destroyer (12) also must appear in Nightway. In the afternoon of the last day he (11) visits various groups who, for a small offering ask him to apply his yucca whip to any spots of pain. The lapel on the face of his red mask should be black as it represents 'dark cloud' through which he is to look at one's eyes and thereby to restore defective vision. The mask is an imitation of **yá łičí·ʼ** a reddish abalone shell. He wears a female mask though he is male. The mask is not used for any other purpose. The white border around the lapel represents **tˣó bitˣáláγʷoš** water foam, because he is supposed to 'look through' dark clouds. The wearer of this mask must paint his body red and apply white clay to his hands.

The Ninth Night.

Shortly after sunset four masked men line up in front of the hogan. These are **na·γé·ʼ ne·zγáni** (6) monster slayer **tˣó bážíščíní** (7) born-for-water, **xaščé ʼołťohí** shooting hashch-e (14), and **tˣó neinili·** (8ª) water sprinkler. Monster slayer carries

bibé·ž his knives, black and blue, in each hand; born-for-water carries **xał** a club in each hand, a black one of pinyon, a red one of cedar; shooting hashch-e carries a mountain lion quiver and two arrows; water sprinkler carries a wicker bottle with water. They line up facing the hogan entrance in this order: (see cut).

When they give their call the patient goes out to them and as he faces them they hum a song after which he returns inside followed by 6, 7, 14, but 8[a] remains outside for a while. Inside a prayer is said (by the singer) during which no. 6 uses his knives with an upward motion over the patient giving his call. He uses the black one east, the blue one from the south, then the black one from the west, the blue one from the north.

No. 7 performs in the same manner with his two clubs except that he makes a downward motion. With the black club he motions downward from the east of the patient, with the red one from the south, with the black one from the west, with the red one from the north. No. 14 also performs with his two arrows over the patient. The first arrow he presses from the east, the second from the south, the first arrow again from the west, the second from the north, always giving his call at each pressure.

Just about then no. 8[a] runs inside and dashes water in every direction. After this the masks leave the hogan and return to the **γé·i· bᵃγan** ye-i home where they remove their masks. This ye-i home is a brush corral in which the masks are kept and the dancers undress to daub their bodies as required. The four who just returned to the ye-i home do not participate in the public dances. On this occasion no. 8[a] is **tˣó neinili·** the water sprinkler, whereas he is **xaščéłbai** gray hashch-e in the dances. No. 14 is not a female but uses the leading female mask (4) on this occasion.

After the preceding group has left the hogan **xaščéšžini** black god (5) enters it alone carrying his torch and **náneska·di** slap cakes on the hoop. The cut of his mask shows both the torch and the cakes strung on a hoop. Immediately he applies his sandpainting to the body parts of the patient. After that the sandpainting is erased and blanketed out.

Dusk settles rapidly in the Nightway season so that night has pretty well begun when the next group of these masked personators enter the premises, but do not step inside the hogan. **xašč̓éłtˣiʾí** Talking god (1) leads them. He is followed by **zaxadoʾłžahí** (10) Fringed Mouth, and he in turn by **γą̓·ʾask̓idi·** Humpback (9).

The arrangement is about the same as on the previous day when 1-10-4 had appeared. On this day however the 9-mask is much as the 4-mask was, a mere companion to the 10-mask. This 10-mask requires more than passing notice.

First of all the slight variance in pronunciation which we meet in **zaxado·łžahá** and **zaxado·łžahí** does not present serious difficulties. The relativizing suffixes **-há** and **-hí** resolve themselves into our English 'the one who' and both forms may be used. In this particular name we get **za-** mouth, **xa-** up and out, **do·łžah** which has been curved by somebody... and either **-há** or **-hí** one who. The composite gives us 'the one whose mouth has been hooked out or up.'

The upcurve in the mouth region of the mask should be its distinctive feature and because sandpainting figures of this supernatural show masked faces it should also appear there. Instead the conventional gourd mouthpiece found on masks perhaps is a trifle larger for the **zaxado·łžahá** mask. The tube is then surrounded with a fluff of blue fox which in sandpaintings is indicated by white fuzzy lines encircling the mouth. This is generally accepted by natives to be responsible for the name **zaxado·łžahí** which Dr W Matthews rendered with Fringed Mouth. In a general way this rendition expresses native feeling about the mask and the personality it represents, albeit we should like to know why emphasis is placed on a 'fringed' mouth and not on an 'up-turned hook' of the mouth itself! For the present 'Fringed' Mouth is retained.

It is noted however that in the **cêní·ʒ̨í** 'midrock' branch of Nightway (**ƛé·ʒ̨í**) the **zaxado·lžahá** 'Fringed' Mouth is called and is **zaxado·lžahá bošƙi·ž ɫičí'ígí·** Fringed Mouth of the Red side, or **zaxado·lžahá bini·' ɫičí·'ígí·** the red face Fringed Mouth. The **bošƙi·ž** and **bini·' ɫičí·'ígí·** 'whose side or face is red' causes no confusion, because **bošƙi·ž** refers primarily to the side of the body, whereas **bini·'** considers only the face of the mask. This means that not only the mask but also the entire right side of the body of sandpainting figures and of masked impersonators must be painted red. The other half of the body is black on sandpaintings (see Matthews, Plate VIII, Sapir-Hoijer p. 157 confirm this). The other half of the mask however is blue.

In the **tˣáɫƛá·hʒ̨í** water bottom branch a **zaxado·lžahí bošƙi·ž ɫico·ígí·** Fringed Mouth with a yellow side appears instead of the red side Fringed Mouth. Matthews (Plate VIII) reproduces the body of this figure half yellow, half blue but with a red-blue mask. The late Cane's Son, however, reproduced both masks as we reproduce them here from his drawings.

His thought was that the yellow body part should be reproduced in **bini·' ɫico·ígí·** the yellow face part of the mask. Other singers do not follow him. Matthews' informants (Plate VIII) employ the red-blue face or mask, and Beadway Singer quite recently would not recognize the yellow-blue face on the mask of Fringed Mouth.

Some years ago when gathering data on **ƛé·ʒ̨í** Nightway I asked my informant Slim Curly to direct sandpaintings of some of the more prominent drawings of this chantway. In the set there are two drawings which Curly called **zaxado·lžahí be·'i·ká·h** the sandpainting of Fringed Mouth. One of them is **na·dą́·ʾ bá si-tˣą́·go** 'if a cornstalk is set for them' because the groups right and left approach the cornstalk.

On the right side of the cornstalk a **zaxado·lžahí** is approaching followed by a **xaščé baʾá·d** female hashch-e, then by another **zaxado·lžahí** and female hashch-e, who are then followed by **γą́·-ʾaskídi·** humpback using his cane. In the tier below them the same figures are duplicated so that ten figures all told approach the cornstalk on its right. All four **zaxado·lžahí** are red-black bodied, each female figure carries a basket in her right, a spruce brush in her left hand, because with this she will shake pollen into the basket from the corn tassel and ears.

The same sequence of figures is observed on the left side of the cornstalk, but here the **zaxado·lžahí** are yellow-blue bodied, females and humpbacks are identical with those approaching the cornstalk from its right side. Approach to a central figure like cornstalk, a body of water and the like, must be gauged by the calves of the legs of the approachers. The calves are turned out, shins face the object approached. Matthews (Pl. VIII) ignores this rule and also presents a simplified drawing, whereas Curly duplicates his main figures, the **zaxado·lžahí** of red-black and of yellow-blue bodies. The females merely collect the pollen.

His second drawing is qualified as **zaxado·lžahí be·ʾi·ká·h tˣó bá sˢką́·go** 'when water is set for them'. A center circle of dark water is drawn with rainbow bars at the cardinal points on which the ye-i travel. On each rainbow bar two **zaxado·lžahí** each followed by a female xashch-e are traveling 'sunwise' or, as the sun itself travels: east to south to west, our familiar clockwise course. The females again are provided with baskets and spruce brushes to collect pollen from vegetation, the conventional corn, bean, squash and tobacco plants which have their roots in the central water pool. The ye-i group travels around this water supply to indicate their concern for the proper water supply — rain, mist, snow or other precipitation — which vegetation needs to thrive.

The leading **zaxado·ɫžahí** on the east and south rainbow bars are red-black bodied, whereas the same figures on the west and north rainbow bars are yellow-blue bodied. No **γą̂·'askidi·** hump-back figures are represented in this sandpainting. In both sandpaintings however, as Curly explained, the mouth of **zaxado·ɫžahí** should be curved upward and, to hide this deformity, the mouth and its tube should be covered with fur of some kind, blue or yellow fox fur. In sandpaintings which he presented this deformity is not too discernible. The white fluff surrounding the mouth piece obscures it.

He definitely, in both of his drawings, excludes the yellow-blue face mask on his yellow-blue bodied figures. On these, in his sandpaintings, he employs the same red-blue face prints, regardless of their body colors. This, as he explained, allows the yellow-blue body color, but does not extend this combination to the mask. This must be red-blue only, regardless of the body colors. It is possible as a matter of course, that one class of singers, to which **giši·ñ biγe'** belonged, preferred to have their yellow-blue mask correspond with the yellow-blue body colors of their sandpainting figures, as well as of the impersonator in public appearances.

Possibly too the **zaxado·ɫžahí** Fringed Mouths of **cénî·ʒ̨í** midrock branch are more in demand by the public than those of **tˣáɫƛáhʒ̨í** water bottom branch are. In any event Curly's explanation of the up-curved mouth hidden by a generous fluff applies to the Fringed Mouths of both branches. Moreover he was insistent upon having the right eye-marks curved upward and all figures distinctly show this upcurve on the eyemarks. Possibly this is done because the upcurve on the mouth is practically hidden. Then too **bíčį̨h** his nose piece is set over the mouth and along the seam of the two halves of the face. This nose piece is painted on the face of the mask with white clay in the shape of a small ladder with four pairs of double cross bars.

The bottom of a native basket is cut out and the remaining rim is marked with white zigzag lines all around the outside and then set on the mask. Inside the rim three sumac twigs are braced together to form a cone surmounted by a head plume of downy feathers. The cones on both masks are painted red on the hide covering the twigs. Red **ʼace·łčí·ʼ** tail feathers are attached along the base of the cone inside the basket. The reproduction of the entire figure of Fringed Mouth in sandpaintings and of the trimmings of his mask is based on events recorded in the Night-way legends.

There (Sapir-Hoijer pp. 155-7) it is related that the Visionary, the hero of the legend, had been waylaying a drove of bighorns which suddenly disappeared out of his sight. When he searched again after a long time what he saw was not bighorns, but Fringed Mouth in his mask approaching him. Fringed Mouth did not speak but gave his call at intervals when he stopped.

He was followed by another masked person called **γą̂·ʼaskidi·** Humpback, who also gave his call as he followed Fringed Mouth. Two other calls were heard that of the Talking and Calling gods. As they approached the young man "**ǹʒiye·ʒáhą̂· bikeh ǯidi·-ƛahlá** because he had waylayed them swooned." As he lay there unconscious the group of masked beings went over to him, because they had no intent of taking his life. Rather they desired to make him realise what or whom he had been waylaying. The point which the narrator makes is that "**ǹʒiye·ʒáhą̂· bikeh** they whom he had been waylaying as told were directing 'his present' **ǯidi·ƛah** swooning condition."

Fringed Mouth is in the lead. The rest of the masked personators merely follow him and are present at his restoring performances. He places the young man's bow and arrows on some nearby bush. Perhaps that explains why Fringed Mouth is represented as carrying a bow in his left hand in sandpaintings. At any rate, in this particular episode, he wrests a hunter's weapons from him and thereby makes him and his unbelieving brothers realise that game must not be wantonly destroyed! In Nightway it is bighorn game, elusive, shy, but resourceful!

On this occasion Fringed Mouth employs the horns of a bighorn to restore the young man. Performing over him on the east side he employs a horn with zigzag lightning symbols marked on it. On the south a horn with straight or flash lightning marks. On the west he repeats with the horn and zigzag lightning marks, on the north side again with the straight lightning marks. Regaining consciousness the young man saw four strange beings engaged upon him. One a Fringed Mouth who wielded a horn of the bighorn. The second a Humpback carrying a rainbow on his hump. The third and fourth in masks decorated with twelve eagle tail feathers, Talking and Calling gods, who also stood there facing the young man.

The narrative didn't strike me as particularly important on first reading. More intensive study of the language which the narrator employed in this particular section of his narrative convinced me that he gives us a comprehensive picture of what masked impersonators really represent. Humpback appears to urge Fringed Mouth to do his stunt. Calling god also appears to urge Talking god on to get both Fringed Mouth and Humpback into the picture.

When an explanation is to be offered, Talking god becomes the spokesman, as his name suggests. The other masked impersonators leave explanations to him, they remain silent. It is illuminating to follow the translation (on p. 159): "what do you intend to do to us? For what purpose were you going along after us?" and the rest which quotes the narrator very faithfully. I follow and accept this translation as very accurate and do not hesitate to say that the narrator identifies at least some of the masked persons of this scene as bighorns and thus gives us a clue to their identity.

They may change their garments at will. The young man had followed them as bighorns, here he sees the same beings masked. To demonstrate their power of transformation Talking god removes his old clothes from him and clothes him in garments like his own even adding a mask which he took out of his own mask. That done they transformed themselves and him into bighorns again because they had planned to take him along with them to their homes.

The **γą̂·ʼaskidi·** (9) Humpback wears a basket head dress much like the 10-mask except that horns extend out from it. At the base of the horns **ʼace·łčí·ʼ** red (flicker) tail feathers are secured in an upright position, and **ʼace·ʼ łižin** black tail feathers alternate with the red tail feathers. The lower end of the two horns is painted black, the upper and tip ends blue.

This blue section, like the lower part of the basket rim, is marked off with **ʼaciǹlƛiš** zigzag lightning, **biċáxoníγé·ʼ bini·γé** to show that fear proceeds from him. **ʼaċos łagai** white downy feathers are attached to each tip of the horns to add to the effect the mask should produce.

The young man also noticed that the Humpback was burdened with a load of rainbows which gave him a stooped position so that he had to support himself on a cane. We illustrate the cane, mask and hump of Humpback (9) herewith.

The cane and the hump are quite prominently brought out in Nightway sandpaintings. As a companion to the 10-mask the Humpback should use a cane and display his hump. To display the hump on the impersonator a bent stave is fastened on the back of the man. The stave is covered with a goat or sheep hide and allowed to dry. When dry it is painted black. White lines (see cut opposite) are painted along the side, while the outer curve is provided with rainbow colors, white blue, white, red, white.

When the masked beings had transformed the young man into a bighorn Humpback set out by throwing one of his rainbows in the direction they were to travel. The bighorns stepped on this rainbow and left with him.

This same scene is re-enacted in every nine-night Nightway ceremonial. Talking god (1), Fringed Mouth (10) and Humpback (9) approach the hogan. The patient goes outside to face them and here Fringed Mouth motions over him from all sides and accompanies these motions with his call. No song accompanies this performance of Fringed Mouth and his companions which may be considered the finale of all 'sanctification' ceremonies of Nightway.

Both Fringed Mouth as representative of the bighorns and Humpback as carrier of the travel means of all ye-i hold exclusive and important positions in the entire scheme of masked bighorns. They are chiefly responsible for transforming the hero into a bighorn and then for teaching him the whole Nightway ceremonial. To an extent then these two masks (10 and 9) are responsible that the Nightway ceremonial exists at all.

It is significant too that when Nightway sends its representatives to the corral dance of Mountain-topway none other than Humpback (9) is chosen as chief performer. He takes the crowd by his superb dancing though he never performs as a dancer in his own Nightway exhibitions.

Nonetheless the 1-10-9 group is spoken of as especial **ʼacáłeh** 'first' dancers, not because they dance but probably because they precede the real **ʼacáłeh** who are to appear presently.

The **'acáłeh** First Dancers.

The preceding group of 1-10-9 which has just left the dancing premises in front of the hogan may perform by special request whenever there is a public **na·'akai** of (dancing) 'groups moving here and there,' meaning that masked dancers will appear throughout the night. The dance however must be opened by the **'acáłeh** first dancers, of whom one may choose either the regular **'acáłeh** or the **xaščé'o·γą·n 'acáłeh** calling god first dancers. Both kinds may not appear at the same ceremonial.

Both the regular and the especial **xaščé'o·γą·n 'acáłeh** must be male dancers. Female dancers are excluded. The regular first dancers must paint their bodies and wear two eagle plumes on the side of the mask. Some singers prefer the right, others the left side as the rattle should be on the right side of the dancer, plumes or eagle feathers on the opposite side. There are four of these male dancers: (1) (2) (3) (3) (3).

Number 1 does not dance but leads the four to the grounds. Number 2 wears the leading male mask but is called **xaščé'o·γą·n** calling god and leads the other three male hashch-e (3) in the important **'acáłeh sin** first or opening song in which no omission or alteration may be made in the sequence of the words. The same holds for the **xaščé'o·γą·** **'acáłeh** calling god first dancers. They line up in this order:

(1) (2) (3) (3) (3) (3) (3).

Again no female masks are employed. Moveover the dancers are attired in civilian dress but adorn their masks with twelve eagle tail feathers, the distinctive head dress of calling god. There are six first dancers in this group, as (1) merely inducts them but does not dance and sing the first songs. He faces them as they begin the first songs much like a band conductor, but merely moving from one foot to the other.

The ʼacáłeh ćósí Slim First Dancers.

Once the regular first dancers have opened the night performances a second group known as **ʼacáłeh ćósí** 'slim' first dancers enter the grounds. This group, a large one, seem to open the field of socalled 'district' dancers, meaning that various localities of the reservation have formed dancing groups who will perform on the grounds and match their dancing skill with other groups. The public is the arbiter and may express itself in no uncertain terms, especially when inexperienced groups venture to perform in public.

However, amateurs are scarcely chosen for the **ʼacáłeh ćósí** groups who appear immediately after the first dancers proper and again at dawn to close these minor group performances. They should know their stuff! As a result more attention is paid to these 'first and last slim performers' than to subsequent groups of dancers who follow, or at dawn precede them.

Even here some latitude is allowed for the 'slim' first dancers as it is for the regular ones. The 'slims' may appear as in cut: meaning that six male and six female hashch-e dance in the group. Again calling god (2) is in charge of all (4s) and (3s) while (1) merely acts as an inductor and (8) as a buffoon. Neither of these two actually dance. That is left to the 3s and 4s who manipulate their gourd rattles and spruce twigs to accompany the songs they may sing.

In this configuration male and female dancers alternate. As (2) uses a male (3) mask he should not be followed by another male (3) but by a female (4) mask which does not imply that male (3) and female (4) masks represent a married couple. As Beadway Singer put it 'there are males and females in the natural order, which does not imply marriage.' But the sequence of personators is observed nonetheless.

Menstruant women may not participate as dancers in this

group. For that matter they are barred from the initiation ceremonies, from entering the ceremonial hogan and from entering the ye-i enclosure. The same holds for men, boys and females who have an open sore on their bodies, or even a red spot on their skin. They are practically barred from any participation in Nightway.

As a rule the formation of alternating male and female dancers will be kept up all night long by groups from various localities. At times however a request is made that **ʼacáɬeh ćósí** slim first dancers be performed by males only. In this event the formation is: (1) (2) (3) (3) (3) (3) (3) (8).

This formation too may be kept up all night by various dancing groups. In any event they close the dance at dawn. They should not see the rising sun! Once the performers have de-masked the singer unceremoniously returns the masks to his transportation bag which he straps to his saddle and leaves for his home. If at all possible a singer of Nightway will strive to be in possession of his own set of masks. Otherwise he must borrow a set from a friendly singer and that, at best, is expensive.

Inside Ceremonial.

Nightway also provides for other alternatives. The patient need not go to the expense of having the **ʼacáɬeh** first dancers and the **ʼacáɬeh ćósí** slim first dancers appear in public. After all he may ask for them and that means a big outlay in sheep, since first and slim first dancers, as well as dancing groups from various localities of the reservation do not appear as free of charge dancers. The groups expect a compensation, mostly a mutton to the group.

There is a provision made in Nightway (meaning the entire ceremonial of nine nights) to economize by eliminating the last night's performances in public. It must be a considerable saving, otherwise the plan would scarcely be advocated. They call it **γʷóneʼé xatˣá·l** 'inside (of hogan) ceremonial' or **ƭó· na·ǯéhégo**

xatˣá·l 'mere visiting' ceremonial. Both terms describe this form of a **χé·ʒí** Nightway ceremonial. They emphasize either that the entire ceremonial is conducted within the hogan, or that the ye-i merely visit at camps outside the hogan 'to sanctify' petitioners.

All ye-i (masks) must appear. That is the rule. Yet, as only a certain number of them appear as actual dancers in public, they may easily be eliminated at the close of a ceremonial. The other ye-i perform as usual in sanctifying the patient or others who may request it. Obviously the gatherings at these 'private' affairs will not be as large as when a public **na'akai** or dance is announced. The point is that the masked ye-i must appear, regardless of a public dance by the male or female ye-i. This may account for the opinion that male and female ye-i constitute a minor group of these supernaturals. In matter of fact however they alone are public dancers. Other ye-i perform but do not dance in public.

If the male and female ye-i do not dance the **xaščéłtˣi'í** Talking god (1) and the **tˣó neinili·** water sprinkler (8[a]) boil the **'ał-tˣah ná'í·bé·ž** all night long. This preparation is a ceremonial stew because it is prepared in the course of a ceremonial only. The ingredients are corn varieties, morsels of mutton or venison, tips of cedar, spruce and pinyon branches, leaves of dodgeweed, grama grass and the like. In many cases this stew is taken to remove certain restrictions which have been imposed by the conducting singer of a ceremonial. After partaking of this ceremonial stew the restricted person is allowed to eat any foods that had been forbidden him or her. In Nightway the stew is taken by the patient after dawn and practically closes the 'inside ceremonial.'

Other Uses of Masks.

If a **χé·ʒí** nightway singer receives an invitation to appear in the **'ił nášʒin** corral dance he may choose 1 and 9, or 1, 4 and 4 while he beats the drum and sings. **xaščéłtˣi'í** (1) may not be omitted, but γą̂·' **askidi·**(9) humpback may replace the two female masks (4). If humpback is chosen he carries his cane as usual.

In **diné biníłčiží** Navaho Windway, in **na'aťoe·** Shootingway and in **xo·žóne·** Beautyway Talking god (1) does not dance but leads the two females (4) into the brush corral to exhibit their dances. The masks on this occasion must be borrowed from a Nightway singer. Also talking god's mask must be borrowed whenever the corral is to be marked off with cornmeal. This is the especial privilege of **xaščéłtˣi'í** (1).

In **mą'iží** Coyoteway a group of three ye-i appear (1, 4, 4) on the last day of the ceremonial. One of the female ye-i (4) carries a **mą'i· do·ƛiž** blue fox, which is prepared with care so that it resembles a live one. This he applies to the patient to sanctify him. The other ye-i (4) carries a basket with cornmeal which he applies to the patient as in γé'i·'aš of Nightway. In Nightway (4) carries a white and a yellow ear of corn which he applies to the patient.

According to its legend the three γe-i (1,4,4) appeared at the coyoteway ceremonial. Hence singers of this chantway own these masks and do not borrow them from Nightway.

The **'aćose·** Downway ceremonial does not appear to close its nine-night ceremonies with a public exhibition of masked dancers. Every night however Talking god (1) and **tˣó neinili·** water sprinkler (8ᵃ) appear masked in the hogan and spend some time in dancing there. Both of these do not dance in Nightway as we have seen, but they are called upon for dancing performances in Downway. As this chantway also takes care of eye and throat troubles it is considered somewhat related to Nightway from whom it may borrow these two masks.

Even more closely related to Nightway than Downway is **xaš-čécohe·** Big-godway. It branches off from Nightway at the episode which records the adultery of Talking god with the daughter of **xaščéłčí·ʾ** Red hashch-e both of whom belong to Nightway. Of the two children whom she bore to Talking god one was blind, the other could see but was crippled and had to move sitting on his haunches. Their mother was disgusted with her boys and their father said harsh words to them though later he regretted this. The boys however clung together. The blind boy with sound legs packed his crippled brother with sound eyes on his back and in that way they traveled on.

The theme in Big-godway is to give the boys a normal condition, to straighten out the limbs of the cripple and to restore the eyesight of the blind one. To effect this practically the entire array of ye-i found in Nightway is here introduced in Big-godway to suggest something for the boys and finally find the needed remedy and make them fit members of human society again. That story is beyond the purpose of this monograph which is concerned more with the masks which are found in this chantway. Among themselves the ye-i do not wear their masks but move about as ordinary mortals.

The Big hashch-e (**xaščécohí**) performs at the **tˣáčé·h** sudatory on the first four days as is done in Nightway. He performs over the patient with his own uprights which have been planted around the sudatory. His mask is a blue colored head mask and must be made for him during a Nightway ceremonial. This is on the order of a male head mask (3) except that six instead of two tail feathers adorn the front of the mask. The mask was especially made for the occasion to be used in curing the two boys. As a result **xaščécohe·** has this and the mask of Black god who conducted that first ceremonial for the boys and then gave Big-god the six feathers for his mask decorations.

To perform in such a ceremonial the Big-god impersonator must have previously 'seen' it, meaning that the ceremonial must have been performed over him at some time or other. This restriction in itself is not popular. First of all Big-god is described as a mean and abusive person who did not hesitate to give even Black god, another independent person, a piece of his mind.

It is also known that lightning struck Big-god's bead strand and caused the beads to turn into lizards of various species. The native 'Figurine' complex mentions such lizards and creeping things for Big-godway ceremonial. To say the least individuals steer clear of Big-god and his creeping beings. Not so much in performing Figurine ceremonies of the Big-god branch of that complex, but in avoiding Big-godway. After all Figurine ceremonies are brief affairs and need not employ a mask.

But to perform a Big-godway ceremonial itself is quite another proposal. Few singers are willing to do so. Some twenty or more years ago a friend of mine, convinced himself that he needed a Big-god ceremonial. He set out to find a singer who knew the details. After a long search and much persuasion he finally induced one of his uncles to perform it. It was a 'sweating' ceremonial known as **kǫ'k̓eh xaná·ltˣé·h** 'removing a person from a fireplace.' This sounds formidable and ought to make you perspire, because you are seated over a heated pit and covered with blankets to keep you heated. Though this pit-firing is found in Nightway and other chantways, Big-godway ceremonial is perhaps less considerate in its treatment of the patient and that may have induced my friend to consider it a very 'strong' ceremonial.

Speaking of friends I searched long for an informant who could give me the inside on Big-godway. My own Frank Walker suggested that we try **dáγa· ǹne·zi·** Tall Mustache of **łe·γi' tˣó** 'spring-in-soil' Arizona. Frank was not mistaken. The man stated frankly that he had made a point of sounding various subjects which were disputed among Navaho singers. As an innocent visitor at various ceremonials he was able to gauge what they had learned in their apprenticeship. From that he drew his own conclusions, much as investigators now are not too dogmatic about statements made by one or the other native informant. Whatever is solid and substantiated is chosen. The rest as we Navaho put it is **ʼá·ǯí** on that side. We respect your opinion but don't follow it!

Frank and I were, as a matter of course, concerned about an accurate text of the **xaščʼécohe·** Big-godway legend. Details had to be supplied later. There was no objection to having the text recorded, but our informant gave it as his opinion that among the living few are familiar with the ceremonial. And some years ago, he said, a singer died who was called **tˣáčéhé** sweatbath practitioner because he performed as **xaščʼécohí** big-god. **xaščʼécohí** as we have seen functions only at the sweathouse during the ceremonial.

A number of its ceremonies are taken from Nightway. The **ʼił yaʼi·ltˣá·d** or snapping the face mask off with a sapling is identical in both ceremonials and is operated by the same masked persons as in Nightway (6 and 7). Even the small hoops on the first night are featured and handled by 1, 4, 8 masks. All told the two ceremonials call on the same masks with the exception that Big-god mask performs at the sweathouse.

He may be seen **ʼašλaʼ góneʼ** at the initiation on the fifth night. There is however no **ʼił náščin** brush corral, and **xaščʼécohe·** is not invited to the corral dance. No masked **ʼacáłe·h** first dancers exhibit here and the close of the ceremonial is a very private affair with Blessingway songs practically all night long. Though Black god was the conducting singer on that occasion he can now be asked to appear in his mask on the last day of ceremonies. As in Nightway his sandpainting can be made in Big-godway and Black god applies it on the patient.

An Old Set of Masks in Nightway.

In earlier days curators of museums sought to purchase ye-i

bichai mask sets--geniune sets as a matter of course. But singers and natives knew the amount of labor which the masks required and also knew the regulations governing their manufacture. They should be cut and sewed during a Nightway ceremonial, then inducted for public use at a second ceremonial. No dancer will don a mask unless it is made of genuine buckskin as the ritual prescribes it. Any singer who has gone through the grind of collecting materials and getting the necessary help at these two ceremonials will think twice before he disposes of his genuine set of masks even at a fair profit.

There is an easy way out of the predicament or there used to be when horses were plentiful. You killed a couple of range horses, ate the meat and made a set of masks out of their hides and sold them to this 'peculiar' American at a better profit than you could realise for the whole hide at the trading post. Everybody was satisfied. The trader got your money and sold you a nice bill of goods. You kept your set of masks and natives chuckled over your ingenuity. The museum curator accepted the set of masks as genuine 'made by the Navaho' and perhaps they served the purpose in his museum exhibits. At any rate reproductions in horsehide were made for 'foreigners' but never replaced genuine buckskin sets. In matter of fact the spurious sets go out to the enemy country and can do no harm to the Navaho!

At the time, say between 1906-10, we saw no point in procuring **ǯiš ṫő· bé'élya·ígí·** an imitation set of masks, such as were being made for museums. But when a certain **na·kai xastˣi·niǹ biγe'** Son-of-the-late-Mexican-Man reported to have put a set of ye-i bichai masks out of use because of his ignorance in conducting the ceremonial our friends urged us to try to purchase them. As the set appealed to me for more studies than I had made of masks in 1908, one of the leading headmen of those days agreed to persuade the owner to see me.

If there was a more persuasive speaker in those days then **bé·š łagai ʼí·łʼíníñ** the late Silversmith I do not know. The headmen used to choose him as their spokesman in any affairs with U.S. Government officials. It says much for him that he presented the Navaho side of a problem well and usually carried his point. He had befriended us at the Mission because of the policy of tolerance which Fr. Anselm Weber had adopted and all of us held to be the wisest thing to do for the time being. The Silversmith and Frank Walker, our interpreter, succeeded in bringing Mexican Man's Son here to us for a talk. We lost no time in coming to terms.

The date of the purchase was July 10, 1910 as I recorded on that day. Even then, as now, I wanted the history of this set of masks. Something, I felt then, must have developed in the family to induce them to dispose of the masks and both Frank and the Silversmith induced the owner to tell its story. I have transcribed the names of previous owners into our present orthography, though I transcribed them at the time in the orthography then in use. That matters little.

I found however, that Largo, one of the signers of the Treaty of 1868, had been instrumental in having the set of masks made, six years after the Navaho returned from Ft Sumner in 1868. This would put the date at 1874 in which year the masks were made and inducted into public use. Largo, large, was a Spanish name given to him as Headman of his district and seems to have corresponded broadly to the San Juan River area. In the Ft Sumner and earlier periods Mexican captives were employed as interpreters and these men are largely responsible for the Spanish names given the signers of the socalled Navaho Treaty.

The Navaho themselves never used these Spanish names for their headmen. Spanish interpreters therefore had to employ Navaho names of men when interpreting to Navahos, but their own Mexican names when interpreting to Government officials.

Largo, then meant little to the Navaho, but became his official name in this document of the 1868 Treaty.

At any rate Largo was named by his people **bᵃgod biƺa·ʾ** and since his death **bᵃgod biƺa·niʾ** (the late) Ears-in-his-knees. He was a **x̂é·ƺí** Nightway singer even prior to Ft Sumner years, but had no **ƺiš** masks and other paraphernalia to complete his pouch. He was in the habit of lowering his head between his knees when lost in thought and that habit accounted for his name: Ears-in-his-knees.

Some six years after the return from Ft Sumner a sister of **na·kai xastˣi·niñ** Mexican Man now dead, who was the father of the present owner of the masks, took sick and the family asked Largo to conduct the ceremonial. Possibly too Mexican Man offered to help along in preparing a new set of masks.

In the spring of 1874 they held a **t̓ó· na·ƺéhégo xatˣá·l** just-visiting-sing, in the course of which the new masks were made. At the time in 1910 I didn't understand what this meant nor what the owner added in his further explanations. I made the notes as he gave them in his account in the hope that later the use of the masks would explain what was meant by some of the terms then used by the speaker.

In later years I learned that a just-visiting-sing is a Nightway ceremonial which is also called **yóneʾé** or **γʷóneʾé xatˣá·l** an inside-ceremonial. The prime reason for these terms is that all masks must appear at Nightway ceremonials. If they are not to be exhibited in public or at a public dance they must appear at least 'inside' meaning, inside the hogan, even if some of the masks go out visiting the neighborhood from the hogan. If this kind of ceremonial is held the public knows that no ye–i bichai dance, as we outsiders know it, will take place.

The point is worth while noting. Masks may not be made in private but must be made while one or other Nightway ceremonial is in progress. The new masks may not be used in that particular ceremonial but must be 'inducted' at another one. Largo, then, had to borrow a set of masks belonging to another singer in order to make his new set. The cheaper 'inside' ceremonial suggested itself to Largo, Mexican Man and his sister, the patient for manufacturing the masks. The 'inside' ceremonial could be held at any time of the year, but public exhibitious with the full set of the masks worn by dancers and other personators are reserved for the frost and fall seasons.

That same year then, in fall, they held a second ceremonial over the same patient in which they 'inducted' the new set made in the spring of that year. Largo again was conducting singer, Mexican Man looked after details, his sister was the patient. It isn't custom to trim masks with feathers, colors and markings at the ceremonial in which they are cut and sewed. But at the 'induction' ceremonial every mask is colored and feathered properly so that visiting dancing groups may display them. Let alone that special masqueraders like 1 and 4, or 1, 4, 8, or 6 and 7, or 5 alone and 1-10-9, and so on, as we have pointed out above, may display the new masks.

This display has been the coveted ambition of new Nightway singers since Largo's time. But in that Ft Sumner period Ears-in-his-knees was an authoritative exponent of Nightway. We should therefore be allowed to visualize what his new set of masks meant to the tribe. After six years of Ft Sumner deer hunting was at a standstill for the necessary buckskins. But the Comanches, Apaches, even Pueblo tribes in the neighborhood of the Ft Sumner area may have widened the views of singers in the tribe to other possibilities for their religious paraphernalia, say buffalo and other tanned hides.

Ears-in-his-knees may have prepared himself at Ft Sumner for future emergencies. For example, his (female) face masks were made of buffalo hides and that was especially stressed by— shall we call him – the salesman and the Silversmith? If so, Largo's first exhibit of the masks must have taken with the natives. They requisitioned them as long as he and Mexican Man lived and some time thereafter.

Largo belonged to the **xašƛišni** Mud clan and, because he was large and tall, he was also called **xašƛišni né·z** Tall Mud Clansman which may account for the Spanish name *largo*. When he died his masks went to his nephew known as **xašƛišni né·z bida'** nephew of Tall Mud Clansman who was also known as **xašƛišni 'acidi·** Mud Clan Silversmith, as he followed that trade. When he died the masks came into possession of Castellano, Largo's brother, known also as **'adi·ća'íni** the late Interpreter.

Castellano in turn gave the masks to the son of Mexican Man **ćósí γʷolγêi** who was called the 'Slender One' and, upon his death, they came into possession of the present owner known again as **na·kai xastˣi·nin̂ biγe'** Son of late Mexican Man. He was not familiar with Nightway ceremonial so that the masks had not been used for six years and he was willing to dispose of them. The sister of Mexican Man who had had the first **na·'akai** Nightway dance ceremonial performed over her was still alive on that July 10, 1910.

At the time I may not have realised what these several details meant. Now however they reveal a common tendency to keep any **ǯiš** or pouch within the immediate family group. Largo bequeathed his masks and pouch to his nephew, not to his own sons, and thus kept up the Navaho tradition of uncle-nephew preference. His nephew must have known the ceremonial as did Castellano after him and the Slim son of Mexican Man. But his brother was not interested in being a singer which made the masks and pouch useless to the family. It had to dispose of the set either to a singer or to local whites. It preferred the latter.

The masks and other paraphernalia were contained in a 100-lb. sugar sack. The sack and its contents is called **ʒiš** a pouch. The masks themselves are also commonly called **ʒiš** because most of them are head masks which slip over the head like a bag. A glove, for example, suggests the same concept: **láʒiš** a hand bag or slip. At any rate the pouch was found to be easily strapped behind the saddle and heavy, substantial sugar sacks withstood wear in transportation.

No particular concern is felt for the coloring and trimmings of the masks. They are colored anew for every dance and trimmings are removed after every public performance. Hence, when the man emptied the contents of the bag, the masks showed little of the coloring and were not decorated with feathers or markings. Some, like the female and male masks had been tied together with their thongs. But the following masks were represented:

xaščéłtˣiʾí Talking god (1);
xaščéʾo·γan Calling god (2);
xaščé bᵃkąʾ six of Male god (3);
xaščé baʾá·d six of Female god (4);
γą̂·ʾaskidi· Humpback (9);
zaxado·lžaí bini·ʾ łičí·ʾígí· red-faced Fringed mouth (10);
xaščéšžini Black god (5);
na·γé·ʾ ne·zγání Monster Slayer (6);
tˣó báʒíščíní Born-for-Water (7);

In addition the bag contained a number of kit and yellow fox skins, the fawn bag for Talking god, a variety of tail and downy feathers, bags with color materials, a number of gourd rattles for the dancers, small medicine bowls, any number of crushed herbs in small bags, knives in the shape of stone arrowheads, and a variety of colored corn on the cob.

By comparing this set of masks with the drawings which **giši·ǹ biγeʾ** Son-of-late-Cane had made in 1908, it became clear that a divergence of opinions may be expected among singers because they are not bound by a tribal code or standard to be followed. For example, in the old set of masks made by Largo in 1874 no mask is set aside for **xaščʼéłbáhí** Gray god who is not even mentioned as wearing a mask.

What I learned in later years was, that informants take for granted that the identity of the no. 2 or Calling god mask is known, because the leading mask of the six Male god masks is generally employed by the Calling god who leads the male and female dancers in every public exhibition. Calling god is so much more important than the clown or Gray god is in this public dancing group that the mask of the clown need not be designated as belonging to him. If the leading Male god mask had been designated as the mask of Calling god it is understood that Gray god will use any Male god mask at the last night's performances. What we have in reality then is seven male masks, one of which is set aside for the clown or Gray god who is known by other names as we have already mentioned.

The set did not bring out the difference between the Fringed Mouth of the red and yellow face masks. It provided only for the red faced Fringed Mouth and implied that Largo felt at the time that the red faced Fringed Mouth alone should appear and the yellow faced Fringed Mouth should be represented in sandpainting masks only. Many other singers hold this view. The mask is shown on our frontispiece, the last one in the lower row to your right. The upcurve of its eyelid mark on the mask's right eye is again very clearly shown and may be accepted as the traditional distinctive mark of this mask.

In time we asked **xastˣi·n xatˣa·łí** Mister Singer to look the set over. He was a practicing ye-i bichai singer and a recognized authority on Nightway. His checkup found the set complete except that the **xaščʼéłčí·ʼ** Red god mask (11) was missing. By certain marks which singers make on the masks they may be identified by other singers, let alonc that the materials and method of sewing must be followed to insure their genuineness. The masks responded to every requirement. The female face masks of buffalo hide were particularly appealing.

The accessories were fairly complete except again that the **ʼaćos coh** big downs were missing. These larger downy feathers are sought to decorate the masks of Black god (5), Monster slayer (6) and Born-for-water (7) and are at times in possession of individuals who impersonate these supernaturals. Singers will borrow them when needed until they can add them to their own outfits.

Asked if the outfit could be employed at native performances Mr Singer explained the following. Because the pouch had been out of use for six years, in other words, since the death of the previous owner, a purification ceremony would be necessary for the masks 'for safety sake.' It could be arranged, he said, to use the masks at any dance, if this purification were performed. After that had been done his thought was that foreign ownership mattered little. The masks have not left the Navaho country, since 'you live' here. Had they been taken outside of our homes, who knows! The people wouldn't use them.

When Mr Singer made the offer to 'purify' the masks and make them 'ready or alive' again for public use our advisers agreed, on condition that missing masks, like that of Red god, the big down feathers, and the like, would be added to the outfit whenever we asked its return to us.

The additions were never made. No objections were made to employ the masks at public exhibitions which were much in demand in the fall of 1910. Word came that the set was much sought for both inside and public or outside dances.

Finally, a very good friend of mine, **čá·la· coh** Charley Mitchell, had to use much moral persuasion to induce the singer to return the masks and pouch at all. The singer felt that he had become 'accustomed' to the masks and hated to part with them. The missing articles had not been added as originally agreed. Perhaps too some of the kit and yellow fox skins, gourd rattles, feathers and other equipment had been diverted elsewhere, who knows? Friends in subsequent years asked for this or that mask to be used in corral dances, but guaranteed their safe return. And when later I was kept on the move in research work the mask set became cumbersome. It finally landed in the museum of our St Francis Seminary at Mt Healthy, Ohio.

In Summary.

The legend γé·ʼi· **xazlį́·ʼgi** on the origin of the ye-i may be accepted as independent of chantway and other legends. To the natives it rationalizes how and why the ye-i exist, that they are **diγin dineʼé** holy people, who are immortal, but live in human forms in rocks, caves, mountains and holy canyons.

The ye-i people had failed to speak, they are speechless ones and are therefore called hashch-e they tried but 'failed' to speak. In leaving their face prints for use by the Navaho the legend presents and emphasizes the reason for not 'speaking' in the masks. The ye-i appear in person at ceremonials and the wearers of masks represent them. If so they too should be speechless while wearing a mask.

Some ye-i like Talking and Calling god, Black god, Monster slayer and his brother, Water sprinkler and others are mentioned as appearing in performances of Navaho ceremonials. This does not necessarily imply that their impersonators must be masked for the performances. Many legends skip this point.

Nightway (**ƛé·ǯí**) must present masqueraders of all its ye-i. In matter of fact the ye-i and their **ǯiš** are never separated meaning, that all ye-i who perform here must be masked. It also implies that every individual mask or a representative of duplicate masks must appear in every nine-night Nightway ceremonial.

These nine-night Nightway ceremonials are either 'inside' affairs which do not close with an exhibition for the public. Or they are public affairs in which various groups of First Dancers appear. Some latitude is allowed here in selecting all Calling god dancers and alternating between male and female dancers. In any event Talking god leads them in, but does not perform as a dancer himself.

This leadership in the public dances more than anything else stamps Talking god as the leading masquerader. In matter of fact, the address form used in approaching him *shi-chai* my granduncle, accounts for the name *ye-i bi-chai* ye-i's granduncle, which has been given to the entire exhibition by white residents. The final dramatization more than any preceding acts is responsible for the name.

The Navaho lets it go at that. To the native however, the leader of the First Dancers is Calling god who opens the entire night's performance with three male associates. Talking god steps aside and leaves the field to Calling god who directs the wording of the songs of his companions and those that follow as 'Slim First' dancers.

Just what should be performed in public is left to the patient. The public will often not be impressed with a Calling god who wears the ordinary male mask and its two side feathers. He or she may believe that the First Dancers should all be Calling gods. That requires again that we exclude female masks and only male dancers are allowed. Their masks must be decorated with twelve tail (of eagle) feathers to indicate this especial request. This is thought to be more effective than employing the ordinary male mask with only two side feathers and is kept up all night long. The importance of Calling god is thus visualized.

Male and female masks are largely dependent upon the choice of the patient at least for the final public exhibitions. Gray god always accompanies these groups. The First Dancers proper, four in number must be male masks only. They are inducted by Talking god, but Gray god does not accompany them, Calling god always leads in dance and song of these groups.

The first song must be carefully sung, that is no word may be missed or altered. Songs which follow can be chosen at random by the song leader. But the two words **xa·yá** it comes out, and

na·yá it comes down, must occur in the songs. Evidently this has reference to rainfall for the benefit of vegetation, corn in particular. It may be inferred from this that the masked dance is a prayer for rain. Since Talking god is said to be in charge of corn, as shown by the cornstalk on the face of his mask, we may infer that the prayer is addressed to the ye-i and their leader who have appeared in person during the ceremonial.

The ye-i are believed to be benevolent benefactors of the human race. They form combinations in order to perform over the patient to remove every cause of indisposition. Eye and throat troubles, paralysis and distorted limbs are chiefly in mind. In a combined effort all the ye-i are called upon to assist and masked at that, as if to hide their identity from the source of the trouble.

Witness, for example, the removal of face masks by means of a sapling and cutting them up by the masked Monster slayer and his brother. Or the ceremony in which Red god lets the patient and others look through the eyes of his mask, and the whipping with yucca leashes by several masked personators. All this is unique in Nightway. And, since Big godway adds only its own Big god mask, the ye-i appear here also except for the closing public dance which is not held.

By far the greatest number of masks are featured in these two chantways. Other chantway ceremonials may feature one or the other mask. If they do not provide for these masks among their paraphernalia they may borrow them for the occasion from a Nightway singer.

Navaho singers make no particular mention of the origin of the masks found in the tribe. It is known that neighboring Pueblo tribes also employ masks in their dances. It is possible however that the provenience of Navaho masks dates back for several centuries. If borrowed from one or other neighbor it was found more convenient to forget this point. The tribe as a whole has adopted this attitude so that Navaho masks are today exclusively Navaho.

Chapter Four

The Legend of the
ˀałkéˑˀ naˑˀaši·

The story begins at a place called **ʒiłaga·í ʒi·ˀis** 'one-taps-white-mountain-with-his-toes.' In the east there was a white hill, in the south a blue one, in the west a yellow one and a black hill in the north. These hills surrounded a beautiful farm and here it was that **yołgai ˀaťé·d na·x̂êi coh bᵃkąˀ siļ·ˀ** 'big trotter (wolf) became the husband of white shell girl.' She bore him **na·dą̋·łgai ˀaťé·d** white corn girl, and **na·dą̋·łcoi ˀaťé·d** yellow corn girl, and their parents made them **do·biˀde·λa·di·** 'whom sunlight does not strike.' But, in time, white corn girl gave birth to white corn, yellow corn girl to yellow corn, that is, each girl gave birth to four kernels, four white and four yellow kernels.

na·dą̋·łgai ǯiščį·go after she gave birth to white corn she covered her four children with **tˣó ˀółah náščí·n** 'collected (surface) waters' while yellow corn girl covered her four children with **tˣó biyá·ž** 'water's child' or spring waters. In this manner corn was produced.

čáˀoł xaxa·zlá 'pinyon-spread-out' was known for its abundant growth of berry bushes, such as **ʒiʒé** cedar or juniper berries; **łičíˀi·** squaw bush; **ʒiʒé diťodí** service berry; **ʒiʒé dóƙǫ́ží** sour berry; **ǯilčił** unidentified; **čǫh biná·ˀ** wild rose berries; **či·łčin** sumac berries; **čil na·ˀax̂oi** grape vines or wild grapes. The two **do·biˀde·λa·di·** girls, however, were not permitted to visit this berry patch and the wolf people occasionally brought them berries from these 'spread-out-pinyons.' They did this four times.

Each of these four occurrences aroused the curiosity of the girls, but **ńłči biyáží** 'wind's child' finally whispered the location of the forbidden spot to them. The sisters then decided to go there.

The elder one produced a **ná·či·lid ʼagodí** 'stubby rainbow' on which she and her younger sister glided along (**ʼálíle·**) supernaturally over hills, valleys and canyons until, about noon, they reached the berry patch. Here they found a canyon with openings east and west and sheer walls extending up south and north. They glided down into this enclosure and at once began to pick a variety of juicy berries.

Suddenly a bear jumped up just in front of them. They explained who they were and, after they had sung four songs for him, he was appeased and left them unmolested. The older sister's hair was braided with **do·ƛiži·** turquoise and hung down to the ground. The younger girl's hair was braided solidly with **yołgai** 'white shell beads,' and likewise touched the ground. But the incident with the bear made them thoughtful. "We should not have come here, my older sister" the younger girl said. "That's true," the other replied. "We did not do well in leaving our home."

"Let us return home," she proposed to her younger sister who at once agreed. They reduced their supply of berries to a small ball and set out. But scarcely had they made four steps when they noticed the **xalgai xińlá** approaching on **yołgai łį·ʼ**, "white shell horses". (Apparently **xalgai xińlá**, "valley-stretched out," is a secret name for the future roaming Utes, due probably, to their mode of travel on horses in single file. Ed.) "Look, sister, the **xalgai xińlá**, 'Utes' are coming," one of them remarked.

The Utes captured them, **xoʼdi·sná**, "the two were made slaves." They cried when they were captured, and people now weep whenever they are led into slavery. The Utes (**nó·daʼá**) promptly deprived the girls of their wealth in turquoise and white beads, forced them for four days (i.e., years) to hard labor, then finally killed them in their homes in the east. (Informant here adds that this is part of **ʒiłƙiʒí**, "Mountain-topway" but mentions no branch of this chantway, nor does he specifically refer to the bear incident and the Ute captivity. Ed.)

All told the girls had been gone twelve days which here equaled twelve years by our reckoning. Their parents and the rest of the people became alarmed and dispatched the wind and thunder peoples to the cardinal points in search of them. The search was futile, so **tˣíñłái diłxił** and **łikiž,** "Gila Monsters, dark and spotted" respectively, were sent for and asked to use their **ǹdilni·h,** or "touch", "trembling power" in search of the lost girls. That, too, was of no avail.

Next they called upon representatives of divination by **desƚį·',** "gazing" into distances; the **'ą'ą'i·,** magpie and the **tˣáłλáh xa'alé·h** brown or diving heron, who likewise failed to locate the girls. Undaunted by these repeated failures their parents constantly reminded friends and acquaintances that twelve years had passed since the disappearance of the two girls and that something had to be done about it! So they decided upon a last method of divination, the **'ì·sċą·',** listening, for which they selected the **na·γé·' ne·zγání** Monster Slayer, and **tˣó bážíščíní,** "Whom-she-bore-for-water" his brother, to function in this capacity. They represented the **xa'nełnéhe·.** In other words the Monster Slayer and his brother were chosen from "Upward-Reachingway" to "listen in" on this occasion. (Other chantways introduce Monster Slayer and his brother, but here "Upward-Reachingway" specifies its own slayers, quite distinct from those of other chantways. **xa'nełnéhéží,** "Upward-Reachingway-Slayers," they are called. Ed.)

These two supernaturals of Upward-Reachingway proceeded to build a hogan of white and yellow corn, of pollen and vegetation. **na·dą·łgai, na·dą·łcoi, tˣádídí·n, nañse' be· xo·γan 'áda·yi·la·** "They, the people (under directions from the two slayers) made a hogan of white and yellow corn, of pollen and (various) vegetation." Meanwhile the two slayers collected the **bižéƚiš,** "earwax," of **na·ẋêi coh,** "wolf", **našdôi coh,** "mountain-lion", and similar felines to be distributed among the "listeners" in the hogan. They added various **nát^xo'** "eye waters" to strengthen their vision. These, earwax and collected eye waters, the two slayers injected into the ears and eyes of the hogan's occupants in order to strengthen their hearing and sight faculties. Then the two sang songs and set out for the east while the "listeners" remained at attention in the hogan. The two traveled to the ends of earth then known, or the horizon line, where they sat down to listen for any sounds. After some time they discerned a faint sound somewhere near the earth's farthest horizon line. They returned to the hogan for a report of what they had heard only to find that the hogan occupants had not heard a thing.

Listening again on the second, third and fourth mornings they heard the sounds more distinctly, so that, as they reported, a person or persons appeared to be walking toward them. On the fourth morning the sounds were quite close and appeared to come from two whitish objects which produced a noise by rubbing against one another. What they had seen and heard they reported at the hogan. That morning monster slayer had already addressed these bones which had the appearance of skulls with noses pointed towards him; "Are you the two who, twelve years ago, disappeared from here?" The two skulls by rubbing against each other, produced a **ǩa·ž--ǩa·ž**--sound, as if in assent. Monster Slayer and his brother repeated the question four times, always with the same **ǩa·ž** reply. Monster Slayer then picked up the first skull, Born-for-water picked up the second skull and carried them to the hogan.

(In **xa'ne·łnéhe·**, "Upward-Reachingway" this episode of the returning skulls is called **ẋô·di nát́á·ž,** "the-two-returned-at-the-outside (of the hogan)" and definitely accounts for the name of the chantway **xa'ne·łnéhe·** "Upward-Reachingway" the ceremonial which here redeemed two humans from extreme distress. They had reached the limit in their skull forms, but were restored to life again by the ceremonial. Ed.)

At the hogan Monster Slayer ordered two **do·ƙa·ƙe·hi·** "unwounded buckskins" to be laid side by side with heads pointing eastward toward the hogan's entrance. That done he entered with the skull and placed it on the north buckskin, whereas Born-for-water placed the second skull on the south buckskin. A very surprised group of people watched these proceedings. Their surprise was even greater when Monster Slayer repeated his question: "Are you the two who disappeared from here twelve years ago?" The skulls answered by a **ƙa·ž**-sound produced by rubbing against each other. Born-for-water, too, repeated the question and received the same reply. Both then repeated the same question and the skulls answered by promptly rubbing against each other.

Next the Monster Slayer filled a **łe·ċa·ʼ** "earthen bowl" with water, to which he added **cin bóʼoshiʼ** lightning struck wood and **gad niʼe·łi·**, "leaves of Rocky Mountain red cedar." This, informant said, is **ʼana·ʒ̨í** Enemyway, and **xóčǫ·ʒ̨í čil** ghostway herb, a medicine against foreign and native ghost influences. A **bé·š diłxił** "dark flint arrowhead," a **łico** yellow one, **do·ƛiž** a blue one, and a **łagai** white flint arrowhead were inserted into the preparation at the cardinal points.

na·ʼazísé the gopher, was then asked to help along. He left the hogan and soon returned with twenty blades of **cáʼásziʼ**, "yucca." These **dane·smąsgo** were rolled into four balls, five yucca blades to the ball. Monster Slayer then added one ball to the mixture from the east direction. He then **dį·ʼ ńde·ťą** sang four long **xaʼne·łnéhe·** songs, after which the people discussed what was to be done. Of those present the following promised to restore these body parts:

naxosʒ̨ą· xastˣi·n earth man promised to make their right feet;

ʒił'isʒą̂· **xastˣi·n** mountain woman man promised their left feet; **'aciñłXiš** **xastˣi·n** zigzag lightning man promised their right shins; **xaǯilgiš** **xastˣi·n** straight flash lightning man their left shins; **ńłcą̂** **bᵃką'** **xastˣi·n** he-rain man promised **xaćosƙid** **ñšñą̂·ǯí** their right femurs; **ńłcą̂** **ba'ád** **xastˣi·n** she-rain man promised **xaćosƙid** **ñšXaǯí** their left femurs;

ƙos **diłxił** **xastˣi·n** dark cloud man and **'á·h** **diłxił** **xastˣi·n** dark mist man promised to make **xaćí·s** their trunks;

na·dą̂·łgai **xastˣi·n** white corn man promised **xaćid** their sinews; **na·dą̂·łcoi** **xastˣi·n** yellow corn man promised the same.

na·dą̂·' **bᵃką'** **xastˣi·n** **'i·'dê·sį́·ł** **ǯin** male corn man said: 'I'll stand within them' (as their soul);

na·dą̂·' **diǯo·l** **xastˣi·n** round corn man promised **xač́ą̂'ášƙaži** their kidneys;

na·dą̂·' **do·Xiži·** **xastˣi·n** blue corn man promised **xač́í·'** **dado·-Xižígí·** blue (small) intestines;

na·dą̂·' **no·dǫ́zí** **xastˣi·n** striped corn man promised **xaćó·s** **bi-γi'go** **'adiłígí·** their blood veins;

na·dą̂· **'ałtˣas'ái** **xastˣi·n** variegated corn man promised: **ƭá·** **bo'oh** **naxalingo,** "whatever seemed to be missing;"

nañse' **xastˣi·n** vegetation man promised **xakášXo** their pubic hair;

ná·ćíłid **xastˣi·n** rainbow man promised **xaga·n** **ñšñą̂·ǯí** their right arms; **šá** **bíXáh** **ǯiłči·'** **xastˣi·n** sun's temple red streak man offered to restore **xaga·n** **ñšXaǯí** their left arms;

xaco·lγał **xastˣi·n** straight lightning man took care of **xaco·'**, their tongues;

yá **diłxił** **xastˣi·n** sky man offered to restore **xaní·'** their faces; **ǯóxona'ái** **xastˣi·n** sun carrier man promised **xaná·'** **ñšñá·ǯí** their right eyes and **Xéxona'ái** **xastˣi·n** moon carrier man **xaná·'** **ñšXaǯí** their left eyes;

xayołká·ł **xastˣi·n** dawn man **xaći·ći·n** their skulls.

čaxałxe·ł xastˣi·n darkness man offered to restore **xaci·γa·ígí·** their hair;
na·γé·ˀ ne·zγání monster slayer and **tˣó bá ʒíščíní** whom-she-bore-for-water offered to provide **xašƛah** their tallows;
xaščéh bᵊką· male god and **xaščéh ba·ˀá·d,** female god promised **diγiníšdo·λe·ł** that they become holy (or immune).
xaščéłtˣiˀí talking god and **xaščéˀo·γa·n** calling god both promised **xóžǫ́·go náxode·šλí·ł** 'I shall make them pleasant again.'
ˀi·ńiˀ xastˣi·n thunder man restored **xʷi·né·ˀ** their voices;
ńłči xastˣi·n wind man **xagá·l xóžǫ́·go náxode·šλí·ł** said he would restore their walking power again to perfect condition;
tˣádídí·n ˀaški· pollen boy said: **xóžǫ́·go náxode·šλí·ł** I'll restore them to perfect condition, and **ˀańłťáni ˀiťé·d** corn beetle girl repeated this;
są·ą·h na·γái long life promised: **są·ą·h na·γái náxode·šλí·ł** I shall make them long life again;
bikeh xóžó·n happiness also promised: **bikeh xóžǫ́· náxode·šλí·ł** I'll make them happiness again.

This re-dressing, as it was called, began at daylight and was completed about noon. The first one had become a boy, the second one a girl. When they arose they were smaller in size than they should have been. Over their heads they wore something similar to a mask, the boy one of **xoyołká·ł** dawn, the girl one of **naxo·coi** evening twilight. These did not fit properly, and the holy people removed them, blew upon them so that they increased to the proper size. In this manner **xayołká·ł ʒiš silį́·ˀ** dawn had become the mask of the boy. **naxo·coi ʒiš silį́·ˀ** evening twilight had become the mask of the girl. Into these masks the two gave their call: **xawó·ˀ, xawó·ˀ, xawó·ˀ, xawó·ˀ.**

The Masks. The story belongs to **xaˀnełnéhe·** Upward-reachingway and the two are called **ˀałké·ˀ na·ˀaši·** 'two who follow one another' not so much because one always follows the other, but because first they were two girls, subsequently however they were made over into a boy and a girl. The white faced **'ałké·' na·'aši·** is called **'ałké·' na·'aši· 'alą·ʒį' sizíní** the **'ałké·' na·'aši·** who stands in the lead, the yellow, evening twilight faced one, is the **'ałké·' na·'aši· 'aké·dę·' xá·λiž** who was born second. (These names apply to the masks, as well as to the two girls, whose skulls were later transformed into a boy and girl. Ed.) The first mask was made by the sun and is still to be found in the sun's home in the east. The second mask was made by **λáxona'ái** 'moon carrier' and is to be found in the home of **'eszą· náλehé** changing woman in the west. (Whereas sun and moon carrier men are mentioned among the creators of the boy and girl, changing woman is not mentioned there. Ed.)

In my field notes I find that **gišiñ biγe'** used phrases like these: **xacoh γʷolγêi bik̓eh xani'ígí·** One called Stingy directed this story; **tˣó díčí·ni bˣxani' íté** this is a Bitter Water clan story; **ńtį·ʒík̓eh xani'** a witchcraftway story. This **xacoh** person (which is probably short for **bił xacoh** he is stingy Ed.) had claimed a set of **'ałké·' na·'aši· bini·'** faces (as masks, both face and head masks, are called. Ed.) And, to prove his claim, he had asked his people to lower him into a pit where he donned the masks. He then told the people that, for the next twelve years, they would starve, as there would be no vegetation. He then precipitated himself over the cliffs, advising the people that the masks would never again be seen. For this reason **'ałké·' na·'aši·** masks are never reproduced in sandpaintings, on buckskin or other materials. And that is the Bitter Water clan version.

(There may be a point to a **kį·ya'ą·ni's** House-in-caves-clan version which our informant, a **kį·ya'ą·ni** House-in-caves-clan member, offers. Yet the very fact that the latter clan member can offer a true reproduction of the original 'faces' or masks seems to indicate that a strict clan rule, after its introduction into the tribe, could not substantiate its claims entirely against another clan. Otherwise why reproduce socalled forbidden masks which one clan tried to destroy? Ed.)

In this reproduction the faces of the masks are made to represent dawn (white), evening twilight (yellow). The eyes are the conventionl triangular mask eyes. But here the eye borders (**binábąh**) are fringed with turquoise on the white mask, with white shell beads on the yellow mask. These represent their respective eyebrows. Mouth (**bizábąh**) borders are similarly fringed with turquoise and white shell beads. (This is unusual in reproductions of masks. Ed.) The **ñłcą́ na·ǯi·n** 'rain down streaks' are quite common in mask reproductions and therefore offer no exceptional feature for these two masks. The rain droops down from the chin line of the masks in black, double lines. The yellow and white bars at the chin of the masks represent **xayołká·ł** dawn and **naxo·coi** evening twilight. The white faced mask places the white down streak below the evening twilight streak on the mask's chin. On the second mask the yellow streak reverses the order — evening twilight takes the position below the dawn streak on the chin of the mask. A similar reversal may be noted in the white and yellow downy feathers which flank dawn and evening twilight. These represent **ʼaćos coh bi·lbá·ʼ** their collars of large downy feathers.

At the ear positions the white mask is provided with **ñłči diłxił bił xalniʼí** a dark wind which informs him at the right ear; with **ñłči do·ƛiž bił xalniʼí** a blue wind which informs him at his left ear. The yellow mask is likewise provided with informing winds. But here the dark wind is placed at the left ear, the blue wind at the right ear.

The faces of the masks are surrounded down to the chin by a black band of **čaxałxe·ł** darkness, **naxo·coi** evening twilight to represent **tˣádídí·n** pollen (on white mask) **xayołká·ł** dawn (on yellow mask); then a blue band to represent **naxode·ƛi·ž** horizontal blue (of evening skies in the east and morning skies in the west) and an outer band of **ná·ćí·lid** rainbow. The yellow and blue bands of the white mask are braided with **yołgai** white shell beads and **do·ƛiži·** turquoise. The white and blue bands of the yellow mask are wrapped with braids of **yołgai** white shell beads, **do·ƛiži·** turquoise and **báščini** jet and these braids represent **bi-ci·γa'** their hair.

At the right head center of the mask, as worn over the head, there is a yellow ear of corn, a white one at its left. At the base of **na·dą́·łcoi** yellow corn, canary bird **cídi·łcoi biťa'** feathers are **ƛózó·ł be· biƙídesdiz** wound with cotton cord (shown in white). At the base of **na·dą́·łgai** white corn, **dółi· biťa'** bluebird feathers are also attached with cotton cord. These canary and bluebird feathers are also attached at the temples and ears, again with the white cotton cord.

Between the temples and the ears of corn **nańse' noxońlį·ží'** **bićą́·dó descˣa·s** 'various kinds of vegetation spread out from them,' yellow above the right temple, blue vegetation above the left temple. On the yellow mask the yellow ear of corn, the canary feathers and the vegetation are placed on the left side of the mask. In the yellow shrub of the white mask **'ańłťáni· 'áłćí·sígí· sidá** a small corn beetle is seated; in the blue shrub **'ańłťáni· coh sidá** a large cornbeetle is seated (which also holds for the blue and yellow bushes of the yellow mask). Pollen shaken from these corn beetles is strewn over and around these plants.

Facing the masks, an oblong object is drawn in the upper left corner, yellow for the white mask, white for the yellow mask. They represent **dilní** a flute, the body of which is made of large reeds, hence their names: **łóƙa·' coh łico dilní** yellow large reed flute. The reeds are set in **do·ƛiži·** turquoise and the four intersections are likewise indicated by turquoise bands. The flutes are provided with four openings which the operator may open or close with his fingers. At the **bizé·'** **sitˣą̨** mouth piece a **yołgai** white shell bead is set, a **báššini·** black jet at the opposite end.

(Since the flute seems to reproduce the **ló·l, ló·l**-sounds of the corn beetle the connection between the corn beetles seated in vegetation and producing this **ló·l, ló·l**-sound, a lulling sound on a flute suggests itself. Ed.)

In the opposite right hand corner we have another very distinctive feature of these mask drawings. The entire complex is called **na·dą̨· 'asťá·n** feathered corn, regardless of the basic white and yellow colors. If a distinction is made at all one may specify: **na·dą̨· 'asťá·n do·ƛiži· be· xadíťé** feathered corn dressed in turquoise, and **na·dą̨· 'asťá·n yołgai be· xadíťé** feathered corn dressed in white bead, because of the turquoise and white bead decorations on their exterior wrappings.

Inside of these bundles there is a perfect kernelled ear of yellow and white corn placed exactly like the headplumes of corn ears on the heads of the masks – yellow-white on the white mask, white-yellow corn ears on the yellow mask. These **do·xonoťíní** perfectly kernelled ears of corn (informant's pronunciation and interpretation Ed.) designate an 'invisible ear of corn' meaning, that nothing of the cob is visible, because the kernels run in compact rows. Two such ears, one yellow, the other of white corn, are centered in the bundle, **dóli·** bluebird and **cídi·łcoi** canary feathers are laid at their base and wrapped with **ƛózó·ł (ńdaǩą̨)** cotton cord strands laced with turquoise and **yołgai** white bead (as calico and other materials were scarce in those days Ed. and informant). At the tip of both bundles **xiná bićos łagai** live white downs (presumably of eagles in flight Ed.) are inserted, whereas the cross at the bottom represents **cáγádińdíni· bi·' ńzdíťį** 'rock crystal to see inside of it.'

In later field notes I found both **do·noxoťíní** and **do·xonoťíní** for 'the perfect kernelled corn cob.' Some significance is attached to it, there can hardly be a doubt of that. For example, our informant definitely states that a meal of **do·xonotíní** kernels aided a singer in memorizing songs, prayers and the like in Navaho ceremonialism. This by no means implies that the **do·xonotíní** belongs exclusively to this forbidden **ʼałké·ʼ na·ʼaši·** complex but may be found elsewhere also. For example, the **do·xonotíní** perfect kernelled corn ears could be invoked by a singer at any time. Wherever a **xóžǫ·ʒí** Blessingway ceremonial is in progress, he may take his perfect kernelled ears of corn, yellow and white, with him. And, as Blessingway songs proceed, he may pluck a kernel from the ear of corn after each song. After the performance he may call upon a virgin **ką' ádini·** to grind these kernels and make a gruel of it. During the meal, which follows this mush preparation, songs are sung which dedicated the meal, as it were, to its sacrificial purpose and insures safe memorization of songs and prayers. (**do·xonotíní** may be owned by individuals and are highly valued due to their scarcity. Ed)

Whereas any native may be in possession of **do·xonotíní** perfectly kernelled ears of corn, the **na·dą́·** **ʼastá·n** feathered ears of corn belong exclusively to the **ʼałké·ʼ** **na·ʼaši·** masks, for the reason that this corn was raised on one of the sacred farms of the underworld and the underworlds commonly are connected with witchcraft, just as the **ʼałké·ʼ na·ʼaši·** legend and masks are so connected. As the legend of **ʼałké·ʼ na·ʼaši·** belongs to **xaʼnełnéhe·** this Upward-reachingway is called the most potent of chantway ceremonials. These, as a rule, are beneficial in their results of curing bodily ailments, production of rain and vegetation. But these masks would enable their owner not only to produce rain, vegetation and cures of ailments, but also would enable him to produce starvation by stoppage of rain, vegetation and ensuing deaths.

The Stingy-One dramatized this power in his suicide which his clansmen more than likely forced him to take. They forced him to disappear with the masks and our informant correctly infers that no real reproductions of them exist within the tribe. Now and then claims of their existence crop up. Some twenty odd years ago I heard of a set which rumor had was in possession of the wife of the late **ʼadiłdiłí** Gambler-at-stick-dice. This man was a **xó-žǫ·ǯí** Blessingway singer of note. It seemed rather unusual that his surviving wife should come into possession of this family heirloom. Blessingway and ghostway, which these masks typify, represent two opposites, say a positive and negative pole. Besides, this Gambler disclaimed any connection between his Blessingway and the underworlds. Blessingway, he claimed, originated after the emergence. And that settled further argument.

I offered his wife a price for the set of masks at her own terms, but got about as emphatic a refusal to my offer as any woman, native or white, ever could politely make. Even my offer to allow my native messenger to compare my drawings with her originals was flatly refused with a message that the masks could not be used even for this purpose. Her fear, that actual possession of the masks, would incriminate her of witchcraft practices, in view of their well-known scarcity, is understandable, but hardly convinced natives and myself of the real existence of these masks. Of which materials were they made? How used in practice? Questions like these were meant to clarify a rather forbidden field in Navaho witchcraft! Are the masks as potent as claimed? Do they exist? Stick bounding Gambler's wife gave us no satisfaction.

A search was again made when there was a rumor that a certain woman, in the Manuelito, N.M. area, supposedly was in possession of this mask set. Rumors like these disappear in mist or thin air and nothing definite can be established. What we arrive at, from these various investigations is that, if there are any **ʼałké·ʼ**

na·ˀaši· masks in the tribe, the owners, men or women, fear to divulge their existence. The suspicion of witchcraft would immediately follow, regardless of protests of the owners. It seems better psychology, on the part of the owner, to disown them though in view of ultimate detection this may prove a difficult task. The owners, if they wish at all to operate, will probably prefer secret operations. But, after all, I doubt very much if the existence of **ˀałké·ˀ na·ˀaši·** masks in the tribe is really established.

We get a tradition here that **ˀałké·ˀ na·ˀaši·** masks were made in this or that manner. Reproductions in actual materials, like buckskin or buffalo skins, are never mentioned. As a result, the reproductions are mythical and vague. They speak of dawn and evening twilight faces of these masks, found in the home of the sun and changing woman, which hardly allow human mortals to put them effectually into ceremonial use. The result is, that no **ˀałké·ˀ na·ˀaši·** masks are reproduced in sandpaintings or otherwise. They are forbidden in these features of Navaho ceremonialism.

As a matter of course the medicine described in the early part of the story must not have been intended for administering to the two skulls. It was made at the time as a pattern for future use. Thus if one has seen the skull of a native, if one has handled a skeleton or its bones, stepped on or over them, if one dreams of the dead this medicine is applied. The patient's face **ňčí ˀíłˀį** is painted red, after which the medicine is administered with song. This must be done before noon and may not be done after noon.

(The ceremony is exclusively **xóčǫ·ží** ghostway, because of its close connection with death and its shadows. In matter of fact **xaˀnełnéhe·** Upward-reachingway ceremonials are popularly not designated by this name, but simply by **xóčǫ·ží** ghostway. The reason is that any **xaˀnełnéhe·** ceremonial must be **xóčǫ·ží** in the ghostway ritual and cannot be conducted in **diγinkʼehǯí** holyway ritual. Corrections of errors or omissions in songs and prayers, are made in the usual way by **xóžǫ·ǯí** Blessingway songs. Ed.)

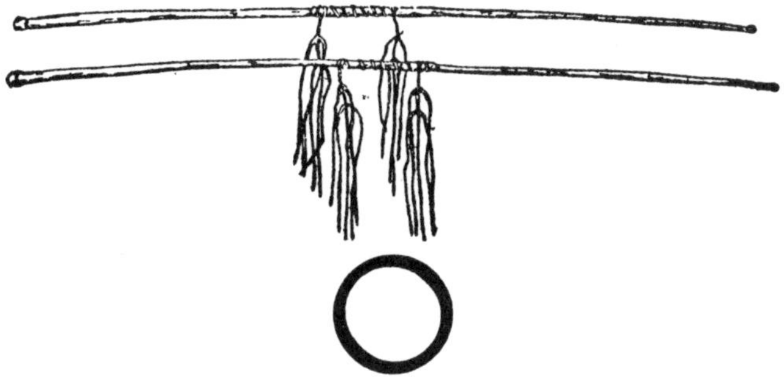

Hoop and Pole

Bibliography

Books pertaining to Nightway are listed on Page 37. Unpublished MSS. on **ʼaćose·** Downway and **xaščʼécohe·** Big-godway, **xaʼne·łnéhe·** Upward-reachingway were also consulted.

APPENDIX

Prayer and Song

of the

ɂacáɬeh First Dancers

ꞌacáłeh bisodizin

First Dancers' Prayer

Part I

céníꞌꞌ xoꞌγandę́ꞌꞌ ḱos diłxił yiḱidahsizíní xaščé bᵃkąꞌ

midrock home from cloud dark upon who stands hashch-e male

xózǫ̂ꞌgo nixił ꞌohkai;

nicely where we are all of you entered;

náꞌčíꞌlid bᵃkáꞌꞌ atˣiꞌndę́ꞌꞌ xóžǫ̂ꞌgo nixił ꞌohkai;

rainbow on it trail along nicely to us you entered;

nixigáꞌl ḱésdongo xóžǫ̂ꞌgo nixił ꞌohkai;

your moving power straight being nicely to us you entered;

nixičíꞌs ḱésdongo xóžǫ̂ꞌgo nixił ꞌohkai;

your bodies straight nicely to us you entered;

nixíniꞌ ḱésdongo xóžǫ̂ꞌgo nixił ꞌohkai;

your minds straight nicely to us you entered;

nixiꞌnéꞌꞌ ḱésdongo xóžǫ̂ꞌgo nixił ꞌohkai;

your voices straight nicely to us you entered;

nixíniꞌ doꞌ daꞌ deiťéꞌgóꞌ xóžǫ̂ꞌgo nixił ꞌohkai;

your minds not anything wrong nicely to us ye came;

nikéꞌlátˣahdę́ꞌꞌ naꞌdą́ꞌłgai nańseꞌ bił ńdińlâi díꞌ

your foot tips along corn white plants with them which lies across these

bił nixił ꞌohkai;

with to us you have entered;

nogod látˣahdę́ꞌꞌ tˣó łah náščíꞌn tˣó biyáꞌž bił ńdińlâi

your knee tip along water collected water's child with which lies across

díꞌ bił nixił ꞌohkai;

these with to us you entered;

nilálátˣahdę́ꞌꞌ tˣóꞌósaꞌ diłxił ꞌacińlxiš bił ńdińlâi

your fingertips along water jug dark zigzag lightning with lies across

dí· bił nixił ʼohkai;

these with to us you entered;

ňcí·s látˣahdę̂·ʼ yódí ʼiłtˣa·sʼái ňXiz ʼiłtˣa·sʼái bił

your bodies' tip along soft goods various jewels various with

ňdiňlâi dí· bił nixił ʼohkai;

lie across these with to us you entered;

nizálátˣahdę̂·ʼ ayá·š do·Xiž tˣádídí·n bił ňdiňlâi dí·

along your mouth tip small bird blue pollen with lie across these

bił nixił ʼohkai;

with to us you entered;

ňci·ká·dę̂·ʼ kʼos diłxił ňłcą̨ bᵃką̨ʼ bił ňdiňlâi dí· bił

along your head surface cloud dark rain male with lie across this with

nixił ʼohkai;

to us you entered;

xǒžǫ̂·go nixił ʼohkai!

nicely to us you entered;

xǒžǫ̂·go šikʼi naxodo·łá·łgǒ·díšní!

nicely me over he'll perform as I say this!

xǒžǫ̂·go šikʼi naxodo·gá·łgǒ·dišní!

nicely me over performed will be as I say this!

xǒžǫ̂·go naxo·ká·ʼ xastˣói danixidínê·łʼį·ł;

nicely earth surface menfolk at us will look;

xǒžǫ̂·go naxo·ká·ʼ sâ·ni· danixidínê·łʼį·ł;

nicely earth surface womenfolk at us will look;

xǒžǫ̂·go naxo·ká·ʼ céłkêi danixidínê·łʼį·ł;

nicely earth surface young men at us will look;

xǒžǫ̂·go naxo·ká·ʼ čikêi danixidínê·łʼį·ł;

nicely earth surface young women at us will look;

xǒžǫ̂·go naxo·ká· ʼáłčíní danixidínê·łʼį·ł;

nicely earth surface children at us will look;

xǒžǫ̂·go naxo·ká· ňdaňťaʼí danixidínê·łʼį·ł;

nicely earth surface chiefs at us will look;

xóžǫ̂·go naxodo·ɫá·ɫgŏ·díšní;
nicely he'll perform as I say this;
xóžǫ̂·go naxodo·gá·ɫgŏ·díšní;
nicely it will be performed as I say this;
są'ah na·γái be· naxodo·ɫá·ɫgŏ·díšní;
long life by he'll perform as I say this;
biƙeh xóžó·ń be· naxodo·ɫá·ɫgŏ·díšní;
happiness by he'll perform as I say this;
ńciží' xóžǫ̂·go nixiɫ 'ohkai;
at your front nicely to us you entered;
niké·dę́·' xóžǫ̂·go nixiɫ 'ohkai;
your tracks along it is pleasant when to us you entered;
są'ah na·γái biƙeh xóžǫ́· noɫį́·go nixiɫ 'ohkai;
long life happiness you are when to us you entered;
xóžǫ́ náxásλį́·', xóžǫ́ náxásλį́·'!
pleasant again, pleasant again things have come to be!

Part II

céní·' xo·γandę́·' tˣádídí·n yiƙi dahsizíní xaščé bˢką'
midrock home from pollen upon who stands hashch-e male
cíɫkę́h xóžǫ̂·go nixiɫ 'ohkai;
youth nicely to us ye have entered;
ná·čí·lid bˢká· 'atˣi·ndę́·' xóžǫ̂·go nixiɫ 'ohkai;
rainbow on it trail along nicely to us ye entered;
nixigá·l ƙésdongo xóžǫ̂·go nixiɫ 'ohkai;
your moving power being straight nicely to us ye entered;
nixičí·s ƙésdongo xóžǫ̂·go nixiɫ 'ohkai;
your bodies being straight nicely to us ye entered;
nixíni' ƙésdongo xóžǫ̂·go nixiɫ 'ohkai;
your minds being straight nicely to us ye entered;
nixi·né·' ƙésdongo xóžǫ̂·go nixiɫ 'ohkai;
your voices being straight nicely to us ye entered;

nixíni› do· da· deiťé·gó· xóžǫ̂·go nixił ›ohkai;
your minds with nothing out of order nicely to us ye entered;

nikélátˣahdę̂·› nańse› na·dą̂·łcoi bił ńdińlâi dí·
your feet tips along plants corn yellow with lies across these

bił nixił ›ohkai;
with to us ye entered;

nogod látˣahdę̂·› tˣó biyá·ž tˣádídí·n din tˣádídí·n bił
your knee tips along water's child pollen din pollen with

ńdińlâi dí· bił nixił ›ohkai;
lies across these with to us ye entered;

nilálátˣahdę·› tˣó›ósa› do·X̌iž xaco·lγał bił ńdińlâi
along your fingertips water jug blue straight lightning with lie across

dí· bił nixił ›ohkai;
these with to us ye entered;

ńci·ká·dę̂·› á·h dilxił ńłcą̂ ba›á·d bił ńdińlâi dí· bił
your head top along mist dark rain female with lie across these with

nixił ›ohkai;
to us ye entered;

xóžǫ̂·go nixił ›ohkai!
nicely to us ye entered;

xóžǫ̂·go šiǩi naxodo·łá·ł!
nicely over me he'll perform!

xóžǫ̂·go šiǩi naxodo·gá·ł!
nicely over me it will be performed!

xóžǫ̂·go naxo·ká·› sâ·ni· danixidínê·ł›į·ł;
nicely earth surface women folk will look at us;

xóžǫ̂·go naxo·ká·› xastˣói danixidínê·ł›į·ł;
nicely earth surface men folk will look at us;

xóžǫ̂·go naxo·ká·› čikéi danixidínê·ł›į·ł;
nicely earth surface young women will look at us;

xóžǫ̂·go naxo·ká·› cíłkêi danixidínê·ł›į·ł;
nicely earth surface young men will look at us;

xóžǫ̂·go naxo·ká· ʼáłčíní danixidínê·łʼį̨·ł;

nicely earth surface children will look at us;

xóžǫ̂·go naxo·ká·ʼ ńdańtaʼí danixidínê·łʼį̨·ł;

nicely earth surface chiefs will look at us;

xóžǫ̂·go šiḱi naxodo·łá·łgŏ·díšní;

nicely me over he'll perform as I say this;

xóžǫ̂·go šiḱi naxodo·gá·łgŏ·díšní;

nicely me over a performance will be as I say this;

xóžǫ̂·go šiḱi naxodo·łâ·gŏ·díšní;

nicely over me as he performs I say this;

są̨ʼah na·γái be· šiḱi naxodo·łá·ł;

long life by over me he'll perform;

biḱeh xóžó·ń be· šiḱi naxodo·łá·ł;

happiness by over me he shall perform;

xóžǫ̂·go tˣâido·ldahgŏ·díšní;

nicely in places going will be as I say this;

są̨ʼah na·γái ʼatˣi·ngó· tˣâido·ldahgŏ·díšní;

long life trail along places going will be as I say this;

tˣádídí·n be· ʼatˣi·ngó· tˣâido·ldahgŏ·díšní;

pollen of trail along places going will be as I say this;

xóžǫ̂·go tˣâido·ldahgŏ·díšní;

nicely in places going will be as I say this;

niké·dę̨·ʼ xóžô·go nixił ʼohkaigŏ·díšní;

in your rear nicely to us ye entered as I say this;

ńcižį̨ʼ xóžǫ̂·go nixił ʼohkaigŏ·díšní;

at your front nicely to us ye entered as I say this;

są̨ʼah na·γái biḱeh xóžǫ́ nołį̨·go nixił ʼohkaigŏ·díšní;

long life happiness ye are as to us ye entered as I say this;

xóžǫ́ náxásλį́·ʼ xóžó náxásλį́·ʼ.

pleasant, pleasant again things have come to be.

Practice varies among singers, but commonly the patient and singer face the masked dancers about like this:

Patient:	Singer:
Calling god (2)	(1) Talking god
Male god (3)	
Male god (3)	
Male god (3)	

The patient repeats the singer's words of the prayer as best he can, but the singer must be careful not to omit any word and must follow their proper sequence. He may not add words to the prayer proper. As a rule the singer says the prayer in a singing tone and pauses briefly after a clause to allow the patient to repeat it. Some singers close their eyes in an effort to help their memory and hurry through the words without interruption. The masked impersonators do not repeat the prayer because it is addressed to the four male gods.

During the recital they sway their bodies slightly and move from one foot to the other until the conclusion of the prayer. The prayer consists of four parts, two of which were recorded. We add a free translation of it here.

First Dancers' Prayer

Male gods from the midrock home, who stand on a dark cloud, it is fine that you came where we are;
It's fine that you came to us along a trail on a rainbow;
It's fine that you came to us with your moving power in straight order;
It's fine that you came to us with your bodies in straight order;
It's fine that you came to us with your minds in straight order;
It's fine that you came to us with your voices in straight order;
It's fine that you came to us with your minds in proper shape;
White corn and vegetation, which are crossed along the tips of your feet, with these you came to us;
Collected rain waters and spring water, which lie crossed

at the tips of your knees, with these you came to us;
A dark water jug and zigzag lightning, which lie crossed along your fingertips, with these you came to us;
Various soft goods and jewels, which lie crossed at the tip of your bodies, with these you came to us;
Blue small birds and pollen, which lie across the tip of your mouths, with these you have come to us;
Dark clouds and he-rain, which lie across the surface of your heads, with these you have come to us;
It's fine that you have come to us;
It's fine that he'll perform over me as I say this;
It's fine that there will be a performance over me as I say this;
It's fine that the old men on earth will be looking at each one of us!
It's fine that the old women on earth will be looking at each one of us!
It's fine that the young men on earth will be looking at each one of us!
It's fine that the young women on earth will be looking at each one of us!
It's fine that children on earth will be looking at each one of us!
It's fine that chiefs on earth will be looking at each one of us!
It's fine that he'll perform as I say this;
It's fine that there will be a performance as I say this!
He'll perform with long life as I say this;
He'll perform with happiness as I say this;
It's fine in front of you since you came to us;
It's fine behind you since you came to us!
All of you are long life-happiness when you came to us!
Conditions are fine again, they are fine again!

Part II

Since there are no female gods in this group male gods alone are addressed.

Male gods from the midrock home, young men, who stand on

pollen, it's fine that you came where we are!
It's fine that you came to us along a trail on a rainbow;
It's fine that you came to us with your travel power in straight order;
It's fine that you came to us with your bodies in straight order;
It's fine that you came to us with your minds in straight order;
It's fine that you came to us with your voices in straight order;
It's fine that you came to us with your minds in proper shape;
Vegetation and yellow corn, which lie across the tips of your feet with these you came where we are;
Spring water and pollen (din ?), which lie across the tips of your knees, with these you have come to us;
A blue water jug and straight lightning, which lie across your fingertips, with these you have come to us;
Dark mist and she-rain, which lie across the top of your heads, with these you have come to us;
It's fine that you have come where we are!
It's fine that he'll perform (a ceremonial) over me;
It's fine that a performance will be held over me!
It's fine that old women on earth will be looking at each one of us;
It's fine that old men on earth will be looking at each one of us;
It's fine that young women on earth will be looking at each one of us;
It's fine that young men on earth will be looking at each one of us;
It's fine that children on earth will be looking at each one of us;
It's fine that chiefs on earth will be looking at each one of us;
It's fine that he'll perform over me as I say this;
It's fine that a ceremonial will be held over me as I say this;
It's fine that he is performing over me as I say this;
He will perform over me with long life;

He will perform over me with happiness one;
It's fine that groups will disperse as I say this;
Along long life trail there will be dispersing of groups as I say this;
It's fine that groups will disperse as I say this!
It's fine behind you since you have come to us as I say this;
It's fine in front of you since you have come to us as I say this;
All of you are long life-happiness I say when you have come to us;
Conditions are fine again, they are fine again!

NOTE

Our records conclude here, but we may reasonably assume that Part III follows Part I and IV follows the alternations found in Part II, then concludes with: Conditions are fine again' repeated four times. After that the patient will strew cornmeal on the masked dancers as an offering and retire to the front of the hogan facing them.

The song leader (2) at once gets ready to begin the ›acáłeh sin First Dancers' Song and is faced by the group leader (1) who urges them on with his call. Perhaps this first song gets more attention than those following it, because of the importance of singing the essential words. A good leader is not long in swinging into action. Shaking the gourd rattle in his hand the other three dancers also shake their rattles and soon the leader intones the burden of the song:

xo-xo-xo-xo-; xi-xi-xi-xí and so on.

At times one catches xa·we, then xa·we ›ížáné which seems to refer to vegetation and čína·dą́·ye bił ní·ya or xa·yá corn comes out with rain. Words like šíxihíwáné bił na·yá are also heard which are said to mean that rain comes down with it. tˣádídį́· bił ní·yá pollen came with it is also heard. Beyond that the meaning of syllables sung conveys little to the listener, though the rhythm of the song and dancers is appealing.

The slim first dancers follow these four first dancers and continue the dances until the first signs of dawn. The singer then makes sure that his set of masks has remained complete.

END OF APPENDIX

A Note on Orthography

Robert W. Young

The alphabet employed by Fr. Berard Haile in the present work is essentially that devised by a special committee of the American Anthropological Association and published by the Smithsonian Institution, in 1916, under the title "Phonetic Transcription of Indian Languages" (Smithsonian Miscellaneous Collections, vol. 66, n. 6), as amended in 1934 to replace digraphs (such as dl, dz, ts) with unitary alphabetic characters (as λ for dl, ž for zh, c for ts).

The practical alphabet in which Navajo is generally written at present differs from the "scientific system" in a number of significant features, as set forth below.

The vowels

Both alphabets employ the same basic letters to represent the vowels of Navajo. These are:

a = the a of father	ai = i in high
e = the e of met	ei = ey in they
i = the i of it	
o = the oa of goat	

However, in Navajo, the meaning is distinguished by contrasting vowel length (short versus long duration), by oral versus nasal production, and by contrasting high and low tone (voice pitch)—including rising and falling tone on long vowels and dipthongs.

Long vowels are written as doublets in the practical alphabet, while length is marked by a raised period in the "scientific" system.

High tone is marked by an acute accent (´) in both systems, while low tone is unmarked in the practical alphabet, and sometimes marked by a grave accent in the "scientific" alphabet. Falling tone is marked by an acute accent over the first letter in a doublet, in the practical system and by a circumflex (ˆ) in the "scientific" alphabet, and rising tone marks the second letter in the doublet versus an inverted circumflex in the scientific usage (ˇ).

Nasality is distinguished in both systems by a "nasal hook" (̨).

Practical

a	á	aa	áá	ą	ą́	ąą	ą́ą́	áa	ą́ą
e	é	ee	éé	ę	ę́	ęę	ę́ę́	ée	ę́ę
i*	í	ii*	íí	į	į́	įį	į́į́	íi	į́į
o	ó	oo	óó	ǫ	ǫ́	ǫǫ	ǫ́ǫ́	óo	ǫ́ǫ

Scientific

a	á	a·	á·	ą	ą́	ą·	ą́·	â·	ą̂·
e	é	e·	é·	ę	ę́	ę·	ę́·	ê·	ę̂·
i	í	i·	í·	į	į́	į·	į́·	î·	į̂·
o	ó	o·	ó·	ǫ	ǫ́	ǫ·	ǫ́·	ô·	ǫ̂·

*Long ii has the quality of i in machine.

Fr. Berard writes the possessive pronoun prefixes ši-/ni-/bi- phonetically as š^{a}-/n^{a}-/b^{a}- before γ/g/k/k̓ when these are followed by a or e.

The Consonants

Practical	Scientific	
b	b	sounds like the deaspirated p in spot
d	d	sounds like the deaspirated t in stop
g	g	sounds like the deaspirated k in skin
gw	g^w	sounds like the gw in Gwynn

/'/	/'/	a consonant produced by closing and opening the glottis. Sounds like the hiatus between huh and uh or between oh and oh in English "huh uh," or "oh oh!" Navajo consonants written in combination with /'/ (k', t', ts', ch', tł') are produced by simultaneously placing the tongue in a k-, t-, ts-, ch' or tł-position, followed by sudden release of trapped air by lowering the tongue and opening the glottis. A "popping sound" ensues. This is the phoneme known as a "glottal stop."
gh (w,y)	γ	a "growling sound" produced by raising the back of the tongue loosely against the soft palate while vibrating the vocal chords. When followed by o gh is strongly labialized and it is written as w in the practical orthography; similarly, when followed by e or i gh is strongly palatalized, and here it is written as y.
w	γ^w	gh + w before e (as in awéé' = aghwéé' / aγ^wé·').
k	k	sounds like k in kick
kw	k^w	sounds like the qu in quick
k'	k̓	see /'/ above
h (x)	x	the "hissing" sound produced by raising the back of the tongue against the soft palate and forcing out a column of air. Sounds like the ch of German nicht. This phoneme occurs only in syllable-initial position. In the practical orthography it is generally written as h.
hw	x^w	sounds like the wh in whoosh
t	t^x	comparable to the t of toe, but heavily aspirated
t'	t̓	see /'/ above
l	l	sound like the l in low

ł	ł	produced by placing the tongue in an l-position and forcing air out laterally, without vibrating the vocal chords
m	m	sounds like the m in man
n (ń)	n (n/ń)	sounds like the n in now. Occurs low or high in tone as syllabic n (comparable to n in n'nen = and then).
z	z	sounds like the z in buzz
zh	ž	sounds like the s in pleasure
s	s	sounds like the s in sis
sh	š	sounds like the sh in she
dz	ʒ	comparable to the dz of adze (but not so strongly voiced. See Navajo d above.)
dl	λ	comparable to the bl of blow if produced with the tongue in the d-position
j	ǯ	comparable to the j in judge (but not so strongly voiced. See Navajo d above.)
ts	c	comparble to the ts in Patsy
tsx	c^{x}	heavily aspirated ts
ts'	ć	see /'/ above
ch	č	sounds like the ch in church
chx	č^{x}	heavily aspirated ch
ch'	č'	see /'/ above
tł	ƛ	ł produced from a t-position
tł'	ƛ'	see /'/ above
w	w	sounds like the w in wish
y	y	sounds like the y in yes